W9-APR-131

debbie travis'
weekend
projects

debbie travis'
weekend
projects

More Than 55 One-of-a-Kind Designs
You Can Make in Under Two Days

by Debbie Travis with Barbara Dingle

Clarkson Potter/Publishers
New York

THIS BOOK IS DEDICATED TO BILL AND WILL—MY HEROES.

Published by Clarkson Potter/Publishers, New York, New York. Member of the Crown Publishing Group.

Random House, Inc. New York, Toronto, London, Sydney, Auckland
www.randomhouse.com

CLARKSON N. POTTER is a trademark and POTTER and colophon are registered trademarks of Random House, Inc.

Library of Congress Cataloging-in-Publication Data
Travis, Debbie.
   Debbie Travis' weekend projects : more than 55 one-of-a-kind designs you can make in under two days / by Debbie Travis and Barbara Dingle.—1st ed.
      p. cm.
   1. Handicraft.   2. Interior decoration.   3. House furnishings.   I. Title: Weekend projects.
II. Dingle, Barbara.   III. Title.
TT157.T724 2000
745.5—dc21
                                                                                          99-087613

ISBN 0-609-60250-0

10 9 8 7 6 5 4 3 2 1

First Edition

acknowledgments

Debbie Travis' Painted House is a television show that is seen around the world. Each week I help a home-owner restyle a room with paint, plaster, paper, and fabrics. Although the walls are the predominant makeover, it's often the smaller things—curtains, cushions, lighting, and accessories—that add the finishing touch. It is these different elements seen and demonstrated on *The Painted House* that inspired this book, and just as on the television show, it is a team effort of wonderfully talented people who bring you all these ideas that you can turn into your own one-of-a-kind pieces.

The creative team at *The Painted House* have an incredible talent for reinventing the most mundane piece of furniture or inexpensive fabric into a unique treasured item. Many thanks go to my art director, Alison Osborne, my designers, Valorie Finnie and Elaine Miller, and my hardworking artists and painters: Pauline St.-Amand, Shelagh Stewart, Susan Pistawka, James Simon, Anne Coté, and Allone Koffkinsky. I would also like to thank the following people who have also contributed their work: Tennille Dix, Penelope Stewart, Debs Brennan, Steve and Kelly Wilkie, Nina Deckert, Andrejs Ritins, Sara Heppner-Waldston, and Bruce Emo.

PHOTOGRAPHY A decorating book needs sumptuous photography that inspires you to tackle these projects yourself. George Ross is the magical eye behind most of these gorgeous pictures. I would like to thank Ernst Hellrung for photographing all the step-by-step instructions. Other photography by Linda Corbett, Richard Poissant, and Peter Sellar.

BEHIND THE SCENES A huge thanks to my assistant, Dana MacKimmie, and her assistant, Stephanie Robertson, for their support throughout the whole process of writing and photographing this book. Also, big hugs to Manuela Hunger and Sophy Cesar.

CLARKSON POTTER Every book needs a great publisher, and I have the best at Clarkson Potter. I offer enormous gratitude to my editor and friend Margot Schupf and I relish the many hours we spend together with purple pencils behind our ears. Thanks to Elizabeth Van Italie, Marysarah Quinn, and Maggie Hinders for making this book look so fresh and user friendly.

BARBARA DINGLE Barbara Dingle puts all my thoughts and passion for this subject into the written word. Although the hours are endless, her enthusiasm and spirit never wane. Thank you, Barb.

TV NETWORKS Special thanks to the many television networks who air *The Painted House* around the world, especially the Women's Television Network in Canada and WGBH Boston and their U.S. public television colleagues. Finally, many, many thanks to all my viewers.

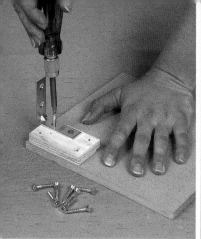

contents

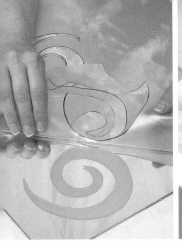

preface

It's often said that it's the small things in life that make the difference. This is particularly true when you are decorating your home. It doesn't matter whether you live in a brand-new condominium, a rambling Victorian house, a tiny city apartment, or a '70s ranch bungalow, it's the personal touches that make it a home. Discovering a unique piece in a Paris flea market or a box of antique leather-bound books in a garage sale makes for an exciting memory and a great conversation. But it's the furniture and accessories that you make and decorate yourself that will become the favorites in your home. These small home projects require no specialized skills, and you certainly don't need much money or time, just an imagination and the ability to let that imagination soar.

All projects in this book can be completed easily in a weekend, which is a great boon given our busy lifestyles. But there is something more compelling about *Weekend Projects.* Painting and decorating furnishings has been popular throughout the centuries, because customizing pieces with paint, gilt, paper, and fabric is not only a way of decorating, but also of personalizing a room. When we move to a new home or change the colors of a room, it's not always affordable or practical to change the existing furnishings as well. *Weekend Projects* will show you how those straight-back dining chairs that looked fabulous ten years ago but don't work with your present scheme can be updated instantly with slipcovers and a painted design. Finding the right coffee table can take forever, and when you finally discover the perfect size and shape, the finish is wrong. That's the easy part to fix. Make it whatever you want. With a free weekend and a trip to the paint store, furniture and accessories can be personalized to suit your particular room.

There are endless ways to reinvent small furnishings and decorative pieces. A laminate shelving unit can be completely restyled with a few lumberyard add-ons and antiqued with paint. You can build and decorate a room screen that not only provides privacy and organizes (or hides) clutter but is a standing piece of art. There are simple upholstery tricks that renew old chairs, and you can create your own unique accent lighting in an afternoon.

One of my favorite pastimes is to examine designer furnishings and try to discover how they were produced, what materials and techniques were used. We are lucky today that most of these once "secret" products are now readily available. A paint finish that used to be done by boiling up resins and glues to make industrial crackle can now be accomplished with a quick trip down to your craft, paint, or hardware store. I hate to sew; I find it difficult to even thread a needle. But with no-sew Velcro and self-adhesive hemming tape, even I can hang curtains or produce a decorative pillow.

My very favorite tools are a brush and a pot of paint. You can use them to achieve any style. If you are intimidated by tackling your walls, floors, or ceilings, then start your journey into decorating by painting a tabletop, making a window blind, or creating a gift for a friend.

Producing your own decorative pieces, whether it's applying a paint finish to granny's old chest of drawers or decoupaging a lampshade, is not just about the money we save. It's also the experience of actually creating something by hand. Life has become a little too fast and technology-driven over the past few years. Take the time to throw down a drop cloth in your backyard on a sunny day and to strip, paint, and decorate an old garage-sale find. I guarantee that by the time you roll into bed, you will have improved your spirit, and that finished piece will not only have a special place in your home, but a special place in your heart.

planning
a project

where to find
inspiration,
ideas, and
the best buys

Shopping for a new table, lamp, or storage unit to coordinate with your existing decor can be a frustrating exercise. However, by using your imagination instead of your pocketbook, you may unearth what you're looking for in someone else's yard sale. You may already own the piece and realize it just needs a little reinventing, or it may be a combination of new and old materials that you put together and decorate yourself.

Today more than ever we are throwing our enthusiasm and energy into personalizing the rooms we live in. Cookie-cutter decorating has given way to an eclectic approach, which allows favorite flea market finds to abide happily alongside new pieces. By applying a few coats of paint to a plain or outdated piece of furniture, you can reinvent it to blend with or enhance any look, from the modern flash of metals and raw steel to the well-worn patina of country antiques.

YARD SALES AND FLEA MARKETS
We live in a time when scavenging is not only acceptable, it's encouraged. Eco-conscious recycling abounds everywhere from city sidewalk sales to country flea markets, and there isn't anything you can't find if you take the time to

look. Secondhand sales are a bargain hunter's dream. Check your local newspapers and supermarket bulletin boards for advertisements; the lists grow tantalizingly long in the spring and fall. I like to plan an excursion, pack a picnic lunch, and drive to the country. It's a great opportunity to take time with a friend or your husband or kids while searching for those hand-painted sale signs tacked up on tree trunks, gateposts, or barn doors.

Whether you are looking for one specific item or browsing for anything at all interesting, it takes a bit of vision to recognize someone else's rejects as something that you can transform into a useful and beautiful object. If you are a novice to this type of shopping, here are some helpful points to consider before making your first purchase. Remember the trusty shopping adage "Buyer beware," but open your mind to the endless possibilities in other people's castoffs.

AUCTIONS AND ESTATE SALES

The large auction houses hold regular sales throughout the year, but you will also find individual auctions listed in the newspaper. They include the contents from offices, hotels, estate sales, and private and company bankruptcies.

Auctions present a more structured setting for a sale. Bidding against others, coupled with the speed with which the auctioneer calls the bids, can be

tips for bargain hunters

• Unless you are able to repair a broken piece properly, or it's worth the expense to have it fixed professionally, leave it for someone else. Check table and chair legs at the joint, look for split or warped wood, pull dresser drawers out and in. No amount of paint will fix a wobbly table.

• Generally, older furniture is better made than newer pieces. Look for unusual shapes. The style of the furniture piece may be out-of-date, but the look can be completely reinvented with a brand-new color or finish.

• Bargain hunting is a great workout for your creative side. When you are sorting through boxes of junk, think about new ways to use old items. Linens, fabric scraps, buttons, postcards, and posters are wonderful stock to have on hand for a new project.

• Prices are rarely carved in stone. It may not be part of the North American cultural genetic code, but try a little haggling. If you really want it and the owner wants to get rid of it, a deal can usually be struck. The best bargains are made at the end of the day. No one wants to move all that stuff back to the garage!

• Allow your kids to browse with you and seek their advice. They are probably better at uncovering hidden treasures and making trades since they do it regularly in the school yard.

very stressful if you are not prepared. But the excitement is intoxicating! Every auction house has a set of rules governing bidding, method of payment, and delivery of larger items. They will take a percentage of the sale plus applicable taxes. Check all this out before you start bidding.

Most auctions give the public time to examine the items before bidding starts. Take advantage of this time and be sure of what you are buying as there are no returns. Sometimes items are bundled together in lots to make quick work of smaller pieces such as empty frames, less valuable artwork, lamps, or linens. Attend a few auctions just as an observer to get the feeling of the event, and when you do go to buy, pick less popular times, as fewer bidders mean better bargains. Do set a monetary limit for yourself and bring someone with you to ensure you stick to it. You will be shocked at how quickly a price can escalate when two stubborn bidders both want the same piece. The auctioneer will be delighted, but it's not worth the letdown when you are back home and review the inflated cost of your purchases in the sober light of day.

RECYCLED BUILDING MATERIALS

Recycling is not just for finished furniture and accessories. When old buildings are demolished, there is usually a fascinating array of salvagable lumber and decorative details such as interior and exterior trimwork, moldings, carved brackets, mantels, doors, window frames, stained glass, and even floorboards and slabs of marble. It's doubtful that you would be able to "shop" on site for these, but there are businesses that specialize in demolition and resale. Once again, use your imagination to reinvent useful purposes for your finds. Gingerbread porch brackets make artful shelf supports. Old metal grating or an ornate piece of ironwork topped with a piece of glass cut to size can function as a table. Apart from the challenge of unearthing unusual accents for your home, it's a delight to retain a bit of history. How and where you found it and fixed it up always makes a great story.

RAW FURNITURE AND ACCESSORIES

If you would prefer to buy new furniture, you can still save money by purchasing unfinished pieces which can be individualized to fit your home's decor.

More and more retailers are taking advantage of the rising interest in home decorating and now sell whole furniture lines that are ready to paint or stain. One advantage of these pieces is that there is little or no preparation work for you to do except applying a coat of primer.

Hardware, craft, and lighting stores carry a growing variety of accessories such as trays, lamp bases and shades, decorative shelving, brackets, sconces, candlesticks, pedestals, and wicker furniture in their raw state, ready for you to finish. These pieces can be constructed of wood, fiberboard, plaster, paper, foam, or basket weave. The exciting news is that you can decorate any of these materials with paint. (See the preparation chart on pages 44–45.)

LOOK AROUND YOUR HOME

Have you ever been so impressed with a product's packaging that you couldn't throw it away? Some manufacturers have turned their containers and wrappings into an art form. It's possible to recycle these as well. Save the delicate tissue cookie wraps for a decoupage project, or a gorgeous Italian olive oil can for a lamp base. Cotton or burlap bags imprinted with interesting manufacturer's labels can be sewn into novel cushions.

Search out reusable decorating materials around your home such as wine labels, postcards, ends of wallpaper rolls, stamps, and buttons. You most likely have enough on hand to begin a project today.

Perhaps the old table in the kitchen or the bedroom set and lamps stashed in the attic aren't ready for the trash bin just yet. Don't let an unappealing color or even a dated style dishearten you as these can be remedied quickly with a fresh painted finish. The same surfaces can also be transformed with a motif of glass tiles or a layer of paper and paste. In the following pages you will find a unique collection of ideas just waiting to be put to good use.

It's amazing what you can come up with when you shop with imagination. One recycled bicycle wheel, some old cutlery, and a set of tin ice cream cups make quite a unique and serviceable chandelier for outdoor dining.

how to build your own projects

I am not nearly as adventurous with carpenters' tools as I am with a paintbrush. Power tools frighten me, and I am all thumbs with a hammer. But over the past few years, working alongside my clever team on *The Painted House,* I have learned some basic skills that have opened up a world of new options. When I can't find the screen or frame I want, now I can build it myself. And this is possible for amateurs like me because so many products and kits are now readily available that make furniture building simple.

WHAT'S AVAILABLE

Take a tour around your local lumberyard, hardware and plumbing store, or home-improvement center to see how easy and economical the retailers have made it to do it yourself.

Ornamental molding and fretwork can be bought by the measure and are an inexpensive way of adding detail to a plain surface. Molding comes in an enormous variety of shapes and is usually sold in 8-foot lengths. The cost depends on the material it's made of, whether wood, medium-density fiberboard (MDF), or plastic or foam. Although designed to be used as wall or window trim, these moldings are ideal for making frames and adding ornamental detail to plain furniture.

Doweling or dowel rods are rounded lengths of wood that can be used for hanging curtains and canopies. Decorative finials finish off the dowels or can top a bedpost.

Medium-density fiberboard (MDF) is an exciting new alternative to plywood and is less expensive and more environmentally friendly than solid wood as far fewer trees are used. It is manufactured from recycled wood fibers, bonded together with synthetic resins, wax, and formaldehyde. It is easier to cut than plywood, gives a neat edge, and has a silky smooth surface, which makes it a dream for painting. Because there is no grain, it is not ideal to be stained unless you use an opaque rather than a semitransparent stain. MDF is dense and takes a little more muscle power to drill. There is also a bendable MDF available, sometimes called wiggle board, which allows you to design curved pieces. A mask should always be worn when cutting MDF as the dust can be toxic.

Rolls of metal mesh or chicken wire come in various patterns and thicknesses. Tin and copper are purchased by the sheet. Sheets of glass and mirror come in precut sizes or can be cut to size at home with the appropriate tools. You'll find pedestals in plaster, wood, foam core, and wrought iron that make perfect table bases. Tabletops come precut in plywood or MDF, or you can ask the store to cut a custom shape for you. They usually charge by the cut.

Iron and copper pipe, S-hooks, and chain make interesting alternate hardware for hanging curtains or bed canopies. There's everything from doorknobs and drawer pulls to metal decals waiting to be used in creative ways other than their original purpose.

Garden centers are also well stocked to help shoppers with project ideas for inside and outside the house.

TOOLS FOR BUILDING

TOOLS FOR BUILDING
1. power drill
2. backsaw (handsaw)
3. miter box
4. jigsaw (saber saw)
5. router
6. multi-tip screwdriver
7. chisel
8. chisel
9. glass cutter
10. tile cutter
11. tin snips
12. nail sets
13. claw hammer
14. rubber mallet
15. staple gun
16. C-clamps
17. adjustable pliers
18. vise grips
19. pliers
20. clamp

The projects in this book do not require many sophisticated tools. It's pointless to spend any money on a table saw or power sander if you are making only one or two items, but a basic tool kit is necessary and will last you for years. Power tools and worktables can be rented if you would like to get the feel before you buy, or if storage is a problem.

1. POWER DRILL A variable-speed reversible (VSR) drill makes quick work of boring clean holes and driving screws into wood or metal. There are a

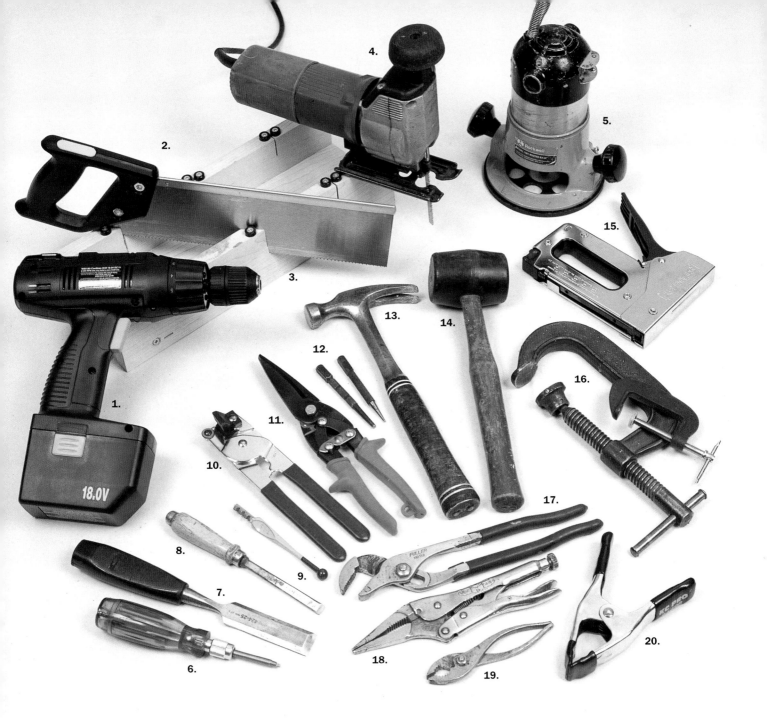

variety of bits sold for different functions: tapered, brad-point, screwdriver, and spade. A must for everyone, a power drill is easy to handle and can be used for everyday jobs such as hanging pictures and other simple household fix-ups, as well as for more challenging woodwork projects.

2. BACKSAW (HANDSAW) A fine-toothed handsaw with a solid spine that runs along the top of the blade to prevent flexing. Used for fine, accurate cuts, mitering, and framework.

3. MITER BOX Indispensable guide for cutting mitered ends on frames, boxing, corner molding, etc. The sides of the box have precut slots that guide your saw so that you can cut 45-degree angles. Used with a backsaw.

4. JIGSAW (SABER SAW) A handheld power saw that can cut smoothly through wood, metal, and ceramics depending on the blade. Jigsaw blades become dull quickly, so be sure to buy spares. This saw cuts curves and fretwork designs.

5. ROUTER A power tool used for adding detail cuts to edges, excellent for cutting reinforced miters and strong joints. Replaces hammer and chisel for shaping wood to take hinges and joinery. A router can be rented, but keep in mind that it takes some getting used to. It might be a good idea to rent it for an extra day and practice before beginning your project.

6. MULTI-TIP SCREWDRIVER This hand-powered screwdriver provides three settings: clockwise, counterclockwise, and lock. It accepts slotted, Phillips (cross), and Robertson (square) tips, which correspond to the design of the screwhead you are using.

7, 8. CHISEL Used along with a hammer to pare away slivers of wood.

9. GLASS CUTTER One end of a glass cutter is used for scoring the glass (use only one stroke to ensure a clean cut). The other end is for knocking the glass once it is scored.

10. TILE CUTTER Same as glass cutter but for ceramic tile.

11. TIN SNIPS To cut wire or metal.

12. NAIL SETS Used to drive nails and brads (small finishing nails) below the surface of the wood, allowing the hole to later be concealed with a filler.

13, 14. HAMMERS While you can make do with one, a variety of hammers is helpful. The claw hammer has a V-shaped notch for removing nails. The rubber mallet does not mark wood as you tap joints into alignment. A small tack hammer has a tiny head designed to start off finishing nails (so you don't hit your thumb).

15. STAPLE GUN Used to secure mesh, chicken wire, and fabric to various surfaces such as wood, plywood, and MDF. A must for do-it-yourselfers.

16, 20. CLAMPS Secure work piece to table for easy, accurate cutting. Hold pieces together while glue hardens.

17, 19. PLIERS For pulling out nails and for twisting and bending wire and metal.

18. VISE GRIPS Adjustable clamping pliers with a quick release.

ADDITIONAL WORKSHOP STAPLES

1. nails
2. corrugated metal wedges
3. screws
4. upholstery studs
5. hinges
6. low-tack painter's tape
7. recoil tape measure
8. set square
9. level
10. colored wax pencil
11. Brackets
12. S-hooks

ADDITIONAL WORKSHOP STAPLES

Depending on the projects you make, you will want to have a backup supply of nails, tapes, and glue. Markers and measuring tools are always needed as well.

There are a number of different glues available designated for specific purposes. Somehow, I always reach for the generic white (craft) glue, and it works for just about everything.

NAILS Finishing nails, called brads, are fine and have small heads. Used to attach trim and thin strips of molding, their small holes are easily covered with a bit of filler and paint.

CORRUGATED METAL WEDGES These are meant to strengthen joints or corners, as in picture frames. They are used along with an adhesive to hold the joins, and hammered in across the join line.

SCREWS Screws have a spiral shank for a strong grip. There are three common heads: slotted, Phillips (cross), and Robertson (square). Check that your screwdriver has the corresponding tip.

UPHOLSTERY STUDS Decorative nails with a short shank used to add detail to furniture and accent pieces. They come separately or in a strip for faster application.

HINGES The most common is the butt hinge, used to hang doors. For instructions on attaching hinges, see the last steps of the directions for building a screen on page 27.

MASKING TAPE Good as an alternative to clamps for holding corners and edges together while glue sets. Also used to protect areas not to be painted, or to temporarily hold down patterns or templates. However, it is very sticky and will pull off plaster, paint, or varnish if the paint is very old or very fresh. Low-tack painter's tape is recommended.

Low-tack painter's tape is also available in light and medium tackiness and is the safest tape to use when protecting areas not to be painted. It has a clean edge and often can be reused. For best results, press firmly along the edge and remove the tape immediately after paint has been applied. Pull it off slowly, toward the fresh paint.

RECOIL METAL TAPE MEASURE The tape has a metal lip at the front end that hooks onto one edge of the object you are measuring while you pull the tape out the required distance to be measured. You can also lock the tape to hold it at a specified length. Some fancy tape measures even compute the measurements.

SET SQUARE RULER (RIGHT-ANGLE RULER) This is used to measure and mark perfect corners.

LEVEL A metal or plastic straightedge with one or two small containers of liquid set into it. The level of the liquid will tell you when your line is straight

—either horizontally or vertically (which is also called plumb).

COLORED WAX PENCIL Available at craft and art supply stores, this pencil has a string below its tip that unwraps more of the waxlike marker as you need it. Good for marking out designs on plastic or metal as it wipes off easily; or on black or dark-colored construction paper as it can be seen clearly.

PENCILS, WASHABLE AND INDELIBLE MARKERS, CHALK All used to mark measurements, positions, and patterns onto a surface. Use an eraser to remove pencil marks and a damp cloth to wipe off chalk and washable marker.

GLUES

GLUE STICKS AND HOT-GLUE GUN This is a fast way to adhere paper, fabric, and other decorative accents to wood. The glue is hot and will burn your skin quickly, so be careful. Do not use on plastic as the heat will melt it.

CARPENTER'S GLUE This multipurpose glue is strong and dries clear. It's used, sometimes along with nails, to bond wood together at joints. Use C-clamps to hold pieces together overnight while the glue dries and sets.

WHITE CRAFT GLUE A good general-purpose glue for adhering paper to paper or wood. It dries clear.

WOOD GLUE This light brown glue is close to the color of wood.

WALLPAPER PASTE Water-based and easy to use for adhering paper or fabric to wood furniture. Apply with brush or sponge. It can be bought ready mixed or in powder form for you to mix with water. It dries clear.

DECOUPAGE GLUE This glue dries clear and is used extensively for decoupage work.

RUBBER CEMENT A pliable adhesive ideal for flexible materials.

SPRAY ADHESIVE Handy for temporary adhesion. Spray onto the back of a stencil before you position it. It is tacky enough to hold the stencil flat, but can be peeled away easily and repositioned.

CONTACT CEMENT (WATER-BASED) This takes more time to use as glue is applied to both surfaces to be joined and there is a waiting period before adhering them. It's helpful to clamp the glued pieces together overnight.

BLUE TACK A sticky material that feels like plasticene. Used to adhere photos or papers to wall. Will not pull off paint or plaster when removed.

three basic building projects

The following pieces use only the most elementary carpentry skills. Once you have learned how to make these simple shapes—a box, a frame, and a screen—you will be able to build any of the projects in this book. And as an added bonus, you might be inspired to create your own unique designs.

work safely
Whether you are picking up a hammer and saw for the first time or you are a seasoned professional, it's good to think about working safely. A new lamp or mirror frame isn't worth a trip to the emergency room!

• Always wear protective goggles when drilling or sawing, and also when cutting glass.

• Clamp wood to be cut or drilled onto a solid worktable or bench to stop slippage. Your work will be neater and the task easier to do.

• Wear a mask when handling stripping chemicals, harsh cleansers and sprays, and mixing powders. Also when cutting and sanding MDF.

• Wear work gloves when cutting and handling glass, mirror, and metals.

• Maintain a tidy work space with enough room to move comfortably.

plywood panel screen

MATERIALS AND TOOLS

- For each panel, ¼" plywood or MDF cut to size
- For frame, ½" × 1" strips of pine, length equal to the perimeter of the panel
- For edges, ½" × 1" strips of pine, to cover the top, bottom, and outside edges of each panel
- pencil and right-angle ruler
- jigsaw
- carpenter's glue
- finishing nails
- hammer
- 2 hinges and screws
- drill
- screwdriver

If you can't find ready-made panels that suit your style of screen, you can put together a screen easily out of plywood or MDF. The latter is an excellent building material, especially if your design has rounded corners or a more complex edge. It is easy to cut with a jigsaw, and, unlike wood, the cut edges will be perfectly smooth.

We used plywood and pine to build two panels and attached hinges to the edges to join them.

INSTRUCTIONS

STEP 1. From ½" pine strips, measure and cut the 4 frame pieces to fit the sides and top and bottom of the panel. (If you want to miter the corners, follow the instructions for the Flat-Faced Wood Frame, page 28.) Measure and cut 3 strips to cover the top, bottom, and outside edges of the panel.

STEP 2. Assemble the panel. Lay the panel flat on your worktable and attach the frame to the front of the panel with carpenter's glue. Glue the edge strips to the top, bottom, and outside edge of each panel so that they are flush at the back and extended above the panel and frame at the front. Once the frame and edge strips are glued, hammer in a few small finishing nails.

STEP 3. Prime and decorate the panels.

STEP 4. Position 2 hinges on the inside edge of the panel. Mark the screw holes with a pencil. Remove the hinge and predrill the holes. When predrilling, it is best to bore a hole slightly smaller and shallower than the screw.

STEP 5. Replace the hinge and screw it into place.

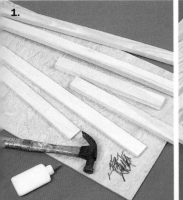

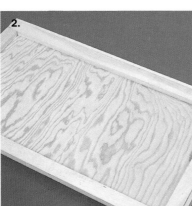

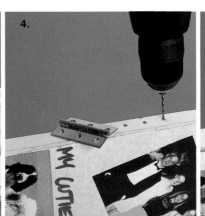

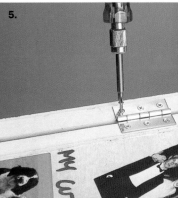

five-sided display box

This common shape is as versatile as it is simple to build. One side of the box is left open to allow you to attach it flush to a wall. You can produce a series of two or three small boxes for displaying keepsakes as I have done with Bombay Boxes on page 102. Alternatively, follow the instructions below and adjust the measurements to fashion a square table base for the Wine-Crate Table shown on page 62. If you are not able to do the cutting yourself, take the measurements for the sides to a lumberyard and ask them to cut the wood.

MATERIALS AND TOOLS

- ⅜" MDF, a piece 18" wide and 4' long is enough for two boxes
- small piece of ½" plywood
- pencil and straightedge ruler
- jigsaw
- medium- and fine-grade sandpaper
- 2 angle brackets and screws
- carpenter's glue
- ⅝" nails
- hammer
- screwdriver
- masking tape
- finishing nails (optional)
- nail set (optional)
- wood filler (optional)

INSTRUCTIONS

STEP 1. Cut 5 pieces from the MDF using a jigsaw or table saw, or take the measurements with you to the lumberyard and have the cutting done there. It is important that the sides are straight so that the box will fit together neatly. For this box the measurements are:

1 piece 8" × 8"

2 pieces 8" × 7⅝"

2 pieces 7⅝" × 7¼"

Also cut 2 blocks from the ½" plywood for the brackets, each 1½" × 2½". Smooth out all the edges with sandpaper.

STEP 2. Lay out the sides in position to form the box: large in the middle, 2 medium sides facing, and 2 small pieces facing. Mark the outside corners of the small pieces for the angle brackets.

STEP 3. To fasten the brackets, glue a plywood block into position on the smallest side at the mark and secure with nails. Screw 1 bracket onto each block.

STEP 4. Before you glue the sides of the box together, fit the pieces into position to ensure that they join properly. If it helps, use some tape to hold the sides in place. This avoids gluing mistakes. To join the box, glue a medium piece to a small piece along one side and tape them together to hold the angle. Run a bead of glue along the bottom edges of this section, attach it to the large

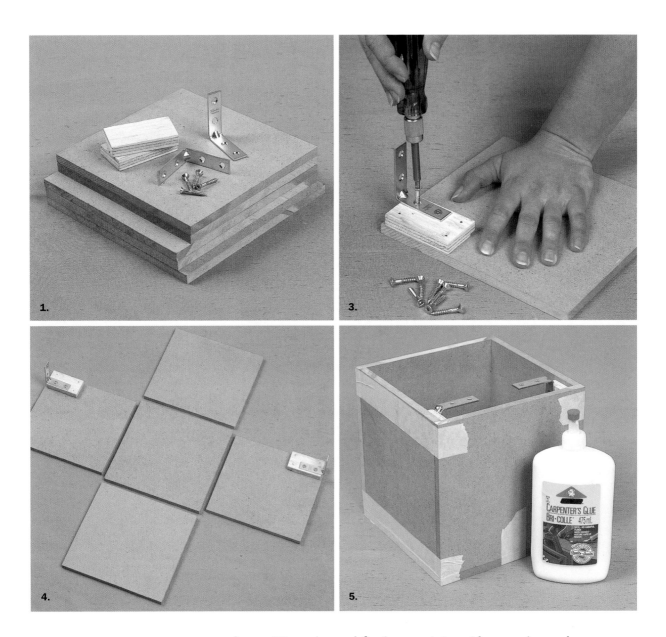

square, and tape. Now glue and fit the remaining sides together and tape.

STEP 5. Allow the glue to set overnight. Remove the tape and decorate the box.

STEP 6. To hang the box, mark the place on the wall where the brackets will be. Put screws in the wall, 1 per bracket. Slip the brackets over the screws. Make sure the screwhead is large enough to lock in position inside the bracket.

OPTIONAL. Finishing nails may be used along with glue to secure the sides. We did not use them here as the box is small, but if you are constructing a larger, heavier piece, then reinforce it with nails. Use the nail set to counter-sink nail heads and fill in the holes with wood filler. When dry, sand smooth.

flat-faced wood frame

The smooth, level surface on this frame makes a perfect base on which to adhere decorative details such as postcards, embossed paper, or mirror tiles as in the Mosaic Mirror on pages 126–27. This is the simplest type of frame to make, and clips are available for attaching mirrors or pictures. Choose plain-faced or smooth-finished soft lumber such as pine or birch. It's available in various thicknesses and is sold by the length.

3.

2.

MATERIALS AND TOOLS

- 6′ length of 1″ × 4″ pine board
- pencil and ruler
- handsaw
- clamps
- miter box
- medium- and fine-grade sandpaper
- carpenter's glue
- masking tape
- corrugated metal joiners (optional)
- hammer
- wood filler
- glass or mirror clips

Mitered corners look more professional and are not difficult to cut if you have a miter box. Remember to reverse the cutting angles so that the sides will fit together. If you are making a frame with strips of molding, it's far simpler to make exact cuts with a miter box.

INSTRUCTIONS

Our measurements are for a frame with an outside perimeter of 60″ (12″ ×18″).

STEP 1. Cut the board in half so that you have 2 strips each a few inches longer than half the entire perimeter, approximately 36″ long. Measure and mark cutting points at 12″ and 18″ on 1 board. Clamp the two boards together, with the marks on the top board, and place in the miter box. Use the cutting guidelines on the miter box to line up the boards. Cutting the two boards at the same time ensures a perfect fit.

STEP 2. Cut through both boards with the handsaw to make the mitered angle. Move the boards to the next mark and cut. Make sure to line up the cuts so that the angles are opposing; they both slant inward. You will finish with 2 lengths that measure 12″ on the long side and 2 lengths that measure 18″ on the long side. Sand the edges smooth.

STEP 3. Glue the 12″ strips to the 18″ strips. Run a bead of carpenter's glue along an angled corner edge and press together. Use masking tape to hold the angles tight until the glue dries.

STEP 4. For added strength, hammer in 1 or 2 corrugated metal wedges.

STEP 5. If the angle fits are not perfect, fill any gaps with wood filler. Let dry and sand smooth.

STEP 6. Decorate the frame.

STEP 7. Lay the frame right side down onto the worktable. Center the mirror or picture face down over the back of the frame, overlapping the open space about ½″. Screw mirror clips to the back of the frame to hold the mirror in place.

4.

7.

working with fabric

Give me a needle and thread and I'm sure my pulse rate skyrockets. When the time comes to cover a window, my department has always been painting and decorating the curtain rods and finials, and even the fabric itself. But watching the design and decorating team on *The Painted House* make curtains and cushions and even upholster dining chair seats without the aid of a sewing machine has put my fear of fabric projects to rest. They create complete makeovers quickly and effortlessly, armed with a staple gun, no-sew tape, and a glue gun!

Simplified methods for constructing window treatments and covering pillows and chairs have become popular and stylish today as the more traditional formality of these treatments lightens up. While there will always be a place for beautifully tailored draperies and trimmed upholstery, alternative solutions are at hand. Anyone can master these easy new techniques.

There is an enormous choice of stunning, expensive fabrics available, and if you require only a yard or so to complete a throw cushion or cover a seat, it may be the place to splurge. But there is also a long list of affordable fabrics: sheers, muslin, linen, synthetic linings, and even sackcloth. Now that textures are so in vogue, these open weaves work beautifully.

No need for complicated hardware. Lightweight sheers are simply looped over drawer pulls that have been screwed into place over the window.

Instead of elaborate valences, curtains can be hung from wooden or metal dowels, ornate finials, clips, and knobs. This look is fresh and young, simple and fun to create. Contemporary architecture and loft-style apartments usually feature vast windows that let in lots of light but offer little privacy. Inexpensive sheers are an ideal solution.

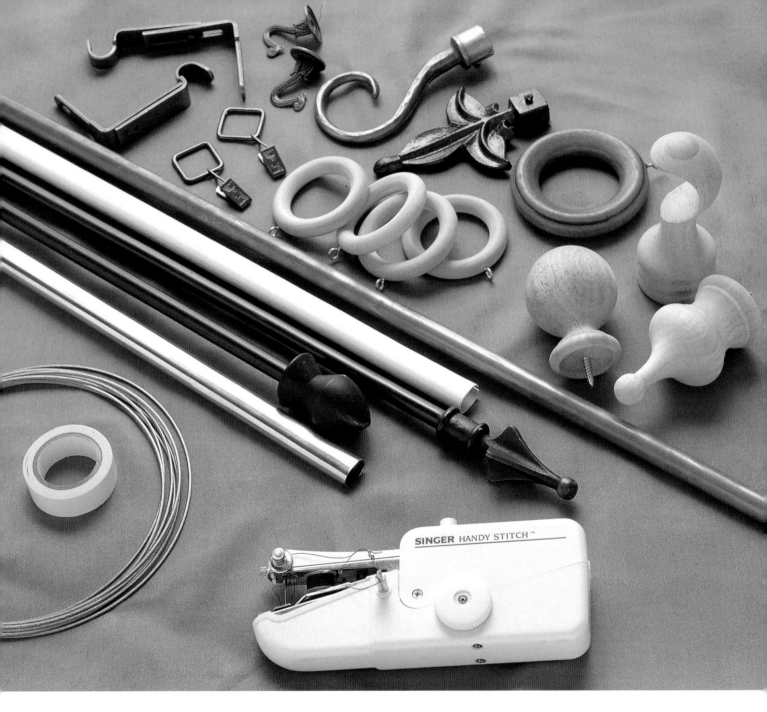

Curtain rods are available at decorating and hardware stores as kits with a finial to attach at each end. Wood or metal finials can be painted to match any decor. Look for decorative hooks, swagging brackets, clips, rings, and wire to have on hand for easy installation.

Slipcovers have become mainstream either to change your look seasonally or as a quick makeover for a dated chair. Customize a set of store-bought cover-ups with a stenciled or painted design, or follow our easy instructions for making and decorating a slipcover for a chair on pages 38–39. Small projects like upholstering a seat require little more than a staple gun, and you immediately have a new look.

Simplified styles are good news for nonsewers. Any pleats, hemming, and trim work can be accomplished with clips, self-adhesive tapes, and fabric glue. Fabric paints, stencils, stamps, and dyes offer unlimited design options. Only one word of warning—working on fabric is a one-shot deal. Mistakes cannot be rectified, so practice first on a scrap of the material you've chosen.

FINISHING EDGES USING HEMMING TAPE

STEP 1. Draw a fold line along the edge of the fabric with a pencil or chalk. Press the tape down using the fold line as a guide. To get rid of excess bulk at the corner edge of the fabric, make a diagonal cut as shown.

STEP 2. Remove the protective strip from the top of the tape and fold the fabric down. The mitered corners will lie flat.

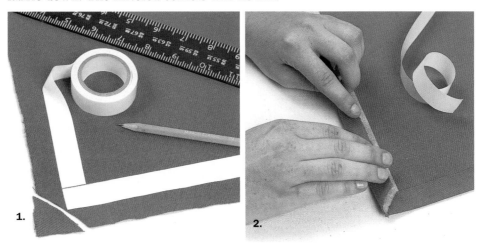

MAKING A HEM OR ROD POCKET WITH GLUE

STEP 1. Fold the fabric down to the inside 1″ and press. Fold the fabric down again, along the hemline, and press.

STEP 2. Run a bead of fabric glue along the 1″ fold and press the hem into place.

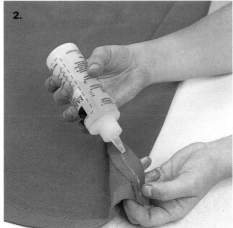

tips for making simple curtains

Whether you are buying fabric by the yard or ready-made curtain panels, you will need to measure the window and wall area to be covered. To create a full look, make the curtains two to three times the width to be covered. Measure the length from the rod to the floor plus 6–10″ inches if you want the fabric to pool; add 8″ for the hem allowance.

Turn under unfinished fabric edges to stop fraying.

Edge seams and hemming can be sewn by hand or machine, or simply held with hemming tape, which comes in a roll and is sticky on both sides, or fabric glue. For side edges, fold the fabric over 1″ and secure. To make a rod pocket at the top of the curtain, fold the top edge over ½″, press it flat, and turn down 3″ or 4″ depending on the size of the rod. Press it flat and secure it with stitching, tape, or glue.

easy accent cushion

There is nothing simpler than sewing up a few accent cushions, and it's a brilliant way to introduce a bit of gorgeous fabric or a bright dash of color into your room. It's just a matter of sewing three straight lines, turning the fabric, and stuffing the shape with fiberfill or a pillow form. The opening can either be sewn up by hand or closed with Velcro.

Examples of beautiful accent cushions are the Pressed Velvet Cushions on pages 162–63 and the Sackcloth Cushions on pages 164–65.

MATERIALS AND TOOLS
- fabric
- tape measure
- ruler and pencil or chalk
- straight pins
- sewing machine or hand stitcher
- scissors
- iron
- fiberfill or cushion form
- needle and thread
- Velcro (optional)

INSTRUCTIONS

STEP 1. Cut 2 pieces of fabric the size of your cushion plus 1″ all around for the seam allowance. On the wrong side of the fabric draw in the seam allowance with a pencil or chalk.

STEP 2. Lay one piece of fabric over the other, right sides facing, edges matching. Pin and sew them together along three sides and around the corners, going about 2″ onto the fourth side. Leave the rest of the fourth side open for turning.

STEP 3. Trim the seams to get rid of any bulk at the corners. Turn right side out and press the seams flat. Turn under the seam allowances on the fourth side and press. Stuff with fiberfill or a cushion form. Pin the open edges together and hand-sew them closed.

STEP 4. Alternative closing: Sew Velcro strips along either side of the opening.

canvas floorcloth

1.

2.

MATERIALS AND TOOLS
- canvas, medium weight
- scissors
- acrylic primer
- 4″ paintbrush
- pencil and ruler
- hot-glue gun and glue sticks
- scissors

You can use either medium or heavyweight canvas to make a floorcloth. The many layers of paint and varnish that you apply produce a strong, serviceable surface. To eliminate excess bulk when hemming the canvas, miter the corners so the cloth will lie flat.

This project forms the basis for the Leafed Canvas Floorcloth on pages 168–69.

INSTRUCTIONS

STEP 1. Cut the canvas to the size of the floorcloth (ours is 3′ × 5′) plus 1″ on all sides for the hem.

STEP 2. Prime both sides of the canvas using a 4″ brush to seal the fabric. Let dry.

STEP 3. Draw in the 1″ hemline with a pencil and ruler. Fold over at the hemline and use the hot-glue gun to secure. Leave just the corners open.

STEP 4. To make a mitered corner, finger-press the hemlines at the corner, but do not glue them down. Open up the fabric and locate the point where the hem fold lines intersect.

STEP 5. Fold the fabric down diagonally at that point, creating two 90-degree angles. Finger-press to mark the line. Open the fabric again and cut along the diagonal.

STEP 6. When folded, the corners now meet neatly, but do not overlap. Repeat for the other three corners and glue in place.

4.

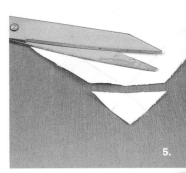

5.

6.

making slipcovers

MATERIALS AND TOOLS

- muslin for pattern, approximately 2½–3 yards, depending on the size of the chair and the width of the fabric
- pencil
- measuring tape
- scissors
- ruler
- straight pins
- canvas, or your chosen material for the slipcover
- thread to match fabric
- sewing machine
- needle
- iron

Most dining or kitchen chairs can be slipcovered but each different shape will need adjustment. This is a general pattern for a straight-back armless chair. It is sewn together in four simple pieces using either a paper or muslin pattern. The method is the same for both. However, a muslin pattern allows you to make a sample and in the end you will have a better fit. If you draw and cut your pattern carefully, sewing the slipcover is quick and easy.

This technique was used to sew the Screen Print Slipcovers on pages 156–57.

INSTRUCTIONS

STEP 1. To make the pattern: Cut a piece of muslin larger than your chair and lay it flat on your worktable. Lay the chair on top of the muslin and trace the outline of the chairback with a pencil. Remove the chair and draw a line 1½″ out from the traced outline along the sides and top and 3″ out from the bottom. This is your cutting line. Cut out the pattern piece and label it BACK.

STEP 2. To make the front pattern piece, measure from the top center of the chairback to the seat and add 1½″. On the BACK pattern piece, measure and mark that front measurement and

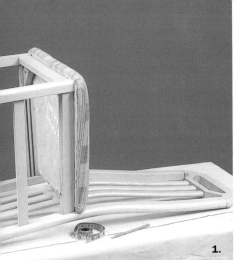

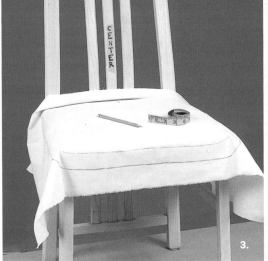

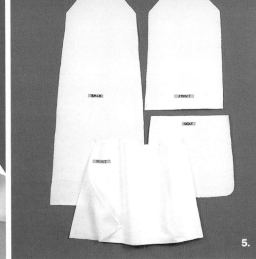

draw a line from side to side. Label this line FRONT. Using your BACK pattern piece, trace and cut out a new piece stopping at the line marked FRONT.

STEP 3. Measure the chair seat and cut a piece of muslin about 6″ larger. Lay the muslin on the chair seat, mark the center back, and with a pencil trace outside the edge of the seat onto the muslin. Lay the muslin flat on your worktable and draw a line 2″ out from the traced line. Cut along this line and label the piece SEAT.

STEP 4. For the skirt, first measure from the top of the seat to the floor and add 3″. This is the height. Now for the width, begin at a back leg, go around both front legs, finish at the other back leg, and add 8″. Cut a piece of muslin to this width and height. Fold it in half. Measure from the outside edge 2½″ along the top. Mark this spot with your pencil. Using a ruler, draw a line from the spot at the top to the bottom corner. Cut along this line so that you now have an angled SKIRT pattern piece.

STEP 5. Pin the pattern pieces together with a ½″ seam allowance, inserting the pins parallel to the edges so that you can slip the cover over the chair and make any adjustments. Once your pattern is correct, cut out the slipcover.

STEP 6. Sew the slipcover together, right sides facing, as follows: Match, pin, and sew together the tops of the FRONT and BACK, leaving the bottom open. Sew the back of SEAT to the bottom of FRONT. Mark the center of the front of the seat piece with a pencil. Also mark the center of the SKIRT (it is at the fold line). Pin and sew SKIRT to SEAT matching centerlines. Pin and sew the side seams of SKIRT and BACK.

STEP 7. Trim and finish the seams. Turn and press the slipcover. Turn under 2″ hem, hand-sew and press.

preparing
your project for
decoration

You've unearthed a fabulous bargain at a flea market, or built a chic set of shelves and a table. Now it's time for the part we'd all like to avoid, but it is essential to a successful outcome. You must prepare the surfaces properly to take whatever finish you have in mind and to ensure that your work will last. Because this preparation is so important, if you are working on a large project that requires a lot of preparation, such as stripping a dresser, my advice is to get it all over with one weekend and then make a fresh start the next.

The preparation required depends on the material the piece you are working on is made of, and the condition it is in. Stripping off old paint and varnish is not a favorite job, but some of the fantastic new primers and sealers now available eliminate or at least minimize the chore. The following chart is a convenient guide for you to follow when preparing surfaces for paint or decoration.

PREPARATION TIPS

Before you start your project, clear a space that will give you enough room to work easily and safely. You most likely will be leaving the project three or more times to wait for paint or glue to dry, and so it's preferable if your work space remains undisturbed from start to finish. Have the tools and materials you require close at hand.

Most of the paints in this book are water-based for easy use and cleanup. But always read the label on any products, and wear a proper mask and protective goggles when appropriate. Protect your hands with latex gloves or heavy-duty work gloves when handling sharp materials such as metal or glass.

Good ventilation is important for you and your project.

CLEANING MATERIALS FOR SURFACES AND TOOLS

In most cases an all-purpose household detergent is all that is necessary. If you require a heavy-duty cleanser such as trisodium phosphate (TSP), wear gloves, have adequate ventilation, and rinse away the cleanser thoroughly. For a more environmentally friendly solution, try white vinegar and water.

Don't soak wood products in water. They are very absorbent and may warp. Once warping has occurred, it is difficult if not impossible to reverse the process.

Paint thinner, also called mineral spirits, is a handy paint and stain remover. Methyl hydrate is a solvent for shellac and for removing hardened latex paint. It dissolves spray adhesive as well as acrylic stencil paint.

REPAIRS

It's a good idea to put together a tool kit to have on hand for common household repairs. You will need a hammer, a screwdriver, various sizes of nails and screws, wood filler and spackle, a spatula, sandpaper, and some clean rags.

WOOD REPAIRS When filling in holes or small splits in wood, use a wire brush to clear away any loose debris and dirt from the opening. Spread wood filler into the opening with a small spatula or putty knife until it is flush with the surface. Let dry. Sand lightly. If the filler shrinks, top up the opening with more filler, let dry, and sand again. Seal repair work with shellac or primer.

If you are replacing rusted or broken hardware, and if the new hardware is a different size, fill in any noticeable depressions and/or holes in the wood's surface with wood filler and sand smooth. If possible, use the same nail or screw holes.

PLASTER Plaster is a soft material and will mark easily. Clean gently with a soft brush and cloth. Pieces of broken plaster can be mended with "super" glues such as Krazy Glue. Fill small cracks and holes with spackle. Sand gently with a fine-grade sandpaper.

STRIPPING

There are a few different methods for stripping layers of paint from wood. They all have their place, but caution should always be used when working with harsh chemicals. Wear protective work gloves, not latex, and a mask, as the fumes are toxic.

Chemical baths or dips can be used for large projects or pieces that have intricate carving, but this method dries out the glues and may permanently alter the smooth working of drawers and doors.

Wood burners are successful for removing thick layers of paint, but care must be taken not to damage the wood, as the burner becomes very hot.

If you want to get down to raw wood, it is much faster, and in some cases safer, to use a commercial chemical stripper. For complete stripping instructions, see Preparing Wood Furniture for Paint on page 47.

SANDING

Warning: If your furniture piece is more than twenty years old and you are not sure what type of paint has been applied, the paint may have lead in it. It is safer and easier to chemically strip the paint away. (See Preparing Wood Furniture for Paint on page 47.)

Sandpaper comes in different grades. The coarsest grade of paper is used to smooth down very rough or poorly finished wood pieces. Medium and fine grades are adequate for most jobs. Fine grade is used for the final touch before painting and in between coats. Sandpaper is sold in sheets. It clogs quickly, so have a good supply.

To make your sanding job easier, wrap a sheet of sandpaper around a block of wood. This gives you something to hold on to, and the pressure on each sanding stroke will be even. There are spongy sanding blocks available that are easy to use and can be rinsed clean of dust. They have a sharp edge for reaching into corners and cracks.

Steel wool is also used to smooth and clean surfaces. It's used with mineral

preparation chart

MATERIALS	CLEANING	REPAIRS	SANDING	SEALER/PRIME COAT
NEW WOOD TO STAIN	Dust and wipe clean with a barely damp rag. Too much water will raise the grain and could cause wood to warp. Allow piece to dry thoroughly.	Fill in any nicks and nail and screw holes with wood filler. It will take stain.	Sand any very rough spots first with heavy-grade sandpaper, then complete the piece with medium- or fine-grade paper. Always work in the direction of the grain. Remove dust with a damp rag, vacuum, or tack cloth.	N/A
NEW WOOD TO PAINT	Clean as for new wood to stain.	Fill in any nicks and nail and screw holes with wood filler.	Sand as for new wood to stain.	Seal with shellac or wood primer. Don't use water-based primer as it will raise the grain. Oil-based primer requires only one coat and you can use latex paint as a base coat.
PREVIOUSLY FINISHED WOOD (PAINTED, STAINED, OR VARNISHED)	Scrape away any loose dirt, peeling paint, or varnish with a bristle brush. If you are stripping the piece down to the raw wood, see instructions on page 43. Clean with soap and warm water, rinse, and let dry. If the original finish is intact, go straight to the priming stage.	Repair any cracks or holes with wood filler.	Sand with fine-grade sandpaper to rough up the surface slightly and give the paint something to hold on to.	Priming is not necessary unless you are changing from an oil-based to a water-based paint or are covering repairs. If you do not know whether an old paint surface is water- or oil-based, rub a small area with nail polish remover. If the paint comes off, it is latex; if the area becomes shiny, it's oil. There are also swabs sold for this purpose.
MDF (NEW OR PREVIOUSLY PAINTED)	Dust and wipe clean with a barely damp rag.	MDF does not nick easily, but fill in any nicks and holes with wood filler.	Sanding is not necessary on a new surface. If you are working on previously painted MDF and the paint has cracked or there are drip marks, sand smooth.	Use a water-based primer on new MDF.
PLYWOOD	Dust and wipe clean with a barely damp rag. Allow piece to dry thoroughly.	Fill in any nicks and nail and screw holes with wood filler.	Sand any very rough spots first with heavy-grade sandpaper, then complete the piece with medium- or fine-grade paper. Always work in the direction of the grain. Remove dust with a damp rag, vacuum, or tack cloth.	Seal knotholes and edges with shellac.

MATERIALS	CLEANING	REPAIRS	SANDING	SEALER/ PRIME COAT
LAMINATE- COATED	Clean the surface with strong detergent, then rinse and wipe dry.	Repair holes and small cracks with wood filler or spackle.	Sand to rough up surface for paint. Remove dust with a rag or tack cloth.	Use high-adhesion primer.
WICKER OR WOVEN STRAW (PAINTED OR VARNISHED)	Remove dirt and flaking paint or varnish with a bristle brush. Remove dust. Wash with detergent and warm water. Let dry completely.	If there are holes in the wicker or areas that are unraveling, you may need a professional to repair the damage. Small pieces of unraveled wicker can be snipped off with pruning shears.	N/A	Use water-based primer, spray if possible, so that the weave doesn't get clogged.
WICKER OR WOVEN STRAW (RAW)	Wash with detergent and water, but do not soak. Let dry thoroughly.	Repair as for wicker that has been painted or varnished.	Sanding is not necessary.	Use water-based primer, spray if possible, so that the weave doesn't get clogged.
PLASTER (FRESH OR UNSEALED)	Use a damp sponge to clean the dust out of the many crevices. Let dry thoroughly.	Repair and fill holes with spackle or plaster of Paris.	Sand and dust gently, being careful not to scratch the surface.	All plaster must be sealed even if you are keeping it white. One coat of primer will seal the surface. If you are making your own plaster molds, fresh plaster takes from 2 to 7 days to dry thoroughly. Do not seal until it is dry.
PLASTER (PAINTED)	Sand off any loose paint. Wipe with a damp sponge and let dry.	Repair with spackle or plaster of Paris.	If previous finish was glossy, sand lightly to rough up surface.	Prime with water-based primer unless previously painted with oil.
FOAM	Dust with a dry brush if raw. If previously painted, remove any loose or peeling paint.	N/A	N/A	Prime with acrylic or latex primer.
PLASTICS	Clean with detergent and warm water or with mineral spirits and steel wool.	N/A	Sand lightly to rough up the surface.	Use high-adhesion primer meant for slippery surfaces.
METAL: TIN, CHROME, IRON, STEEL	Scrape away any dirt and rust. Wipe with mineral spirits and steel wool, then wash with detergent and dry.	N/A	N/A	Use a metal primer to prevent the metal from rusting even if the project is going to be inside.
GLASS	Degrease with vinegar and water and wipe dry.	N/A	N/A	N/A

spirits to clean metal. It is good for working around intricate detail, wicker, and mesh.

When sanding wood, always move with the grain as much as possible to avoid scratching and blurring the surface. Wipe away the sanding dust with a lint-free rag or tack cloth. A tack cloth is permeated with a sticky substance that dust adheres to, making cleanup a breeze. Don't press down too hard when you wipe up the sanding dust or the stickiness will stay behind on your surface.

SEALING AND PRIMING

Porous materials such as wood and plaster require sealing before you apply paint or other decoration to them. If you miss this step, the paint will continue to be absorbed, giving an uneven finish and wasting layers of paint. Likewise, if you are attempting to glue paper to unsealed wood, the water in the glue will be absorbed and won't hold fast. Use shellac and/or a coat of primer for best results. Check the preparation chart on pages 44 and 45 for your project's specific needs.

The two most common sealers are shellac, which is varnish-based, and the primers, which are paint-based. Shellac has many purposes for decorators and artists, but it's most commonly used to seal the knots in new wood. There are all-purpose primers as well as primers designed for metal or shiny surfaces. Ask your salesperson to direct you to the right product for your project and read the label carefully before you buy.

Primers are chemically designed to cling to a surface and make a good base for paint. Today's super-adhesion primers will stick to such shiny surfaces as laminates, melamine, veneers, plastics, and ceramic tile, and also high-gloss paint and varnished surfaces. The huge advantage to high-adhesion primers is that if the original surface is not peeling or blistered, you do not have to strip the piece; just sand enough to rough up the surface.

Alcohol-based primers are your best choice for covering stains that would normally bleed through a layer of paint, such as tobacco, ink, cup marks, and the resins in wood knots. Use methyl hydrate for cleanup.

preparing wood furniture **for paint**

We show here step-by-step instructions for preparing a dresser for paint. These are the steps to follow for readying any wood furniture that is in poor condition. It's a big job, and I always advise you complete this stage one weekend and leave the fun of decorating for the next weekend when you are fresh. To make the process simpler and to ensure a professional, long-lasting outcome, remove all cupboard doors, dresser drawers, and any hardware before you begin stripping and sanding. When working on a chair, turn it upside down to work on the legs. To avoid harming the wood, always rub and sand in the direction of the grain.

MATERIALS AND TOOLS

- screwdriver
- work gloves (not latex)
- chemical stripper
- old paintbrush
- scraper
- stripping pad
- sandpaper
- clean rags
- wood filler
- tack cloth
- alkyd primer

INSTRUCTIONS

STEP 1. Take the drawers out and remove the hardware.

STEP 2. Wearing gloves, brush on chemical stripper with an old paintbrush. Let sit 2–3 minutes.

STEP 3. Remove the residue with a scraper. Use an even pressure when scraping. If you press too hard, you may dent the wood. Instead, repeat steps 2 and 3 if necessary.

STEP 4. To remove hard-to-reach paint from cracks and crevices, brush on stripper and rub with a stripping pad.

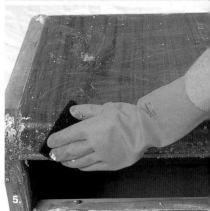

STEP 5. Sand the surface and wipe clean with clean rags. Make sure the surface is clear of any chemical residue.

STEP 6. Fill any holes with wood filler. Let dry and sand smooth. Remove any sanding dust with a tack cloth. You may need a few applications of filler; it's better to build up thin layers than to have one thick layer.

STEP 7. Prime the wood with alkyd primer. Once dry, you can see more clearly if the wood filler is flush with the surface. A further sanding can be done and more filler added if required. If this is the case, add more primer where needed. The surface is now ready for paint.

decorating materials and tools

Change the finish on a piece of furniture and you have instantly changed its personality. Something as simple as a different paint color will give you the freedom to reinvent the style of a dresser, a table, or a picture frame. You don't have to be an artist or a professional refinisher to decorate furniture or home accessories. The paints, glazes, and tools required are all readily available and easy to use. There's also an abundance of other decorative materials to work with that can be used on their own as well as alongside paint. There are beautiful metal leaf and foils, and all kinds of paper products, from wallpaper and colored construction paper to exquisite patterned tissue papers. And decorative plasters are popular once again as a wonderful material for fashioning textured surfaces. Hardware stores also offer an incredible selection of wood brackets, moldings, and ornamental relief work.

It's great fun to apply a new and unique finish to a small project, and far less intimidating than on walls or a floor. For example, a tabletop is like a practice board, and if you're not happy with the results it's an easy job to do over.

If you're covering a large area, such as a chest of drawers, an armoire, or a screen, water-based latex and acrylic commercial paints offer a wide range of colors and are sold in quarts (or liters), more than enough to complete the job.

Craft paints, which are found in art, craft, and some hardware stores, are ideal for small jobs such as trim work or detail or if your project requires small

These are some of the brushes used for creating painted finishes: a badger-hair softening brush, floggers, a stippling brush, various sizes of fitches and a stencil brush.

amounts of many colors. They come in opaque and translucent colors.

You may be ready to work with artist's acrylics. Because the amount of paint needed for a project is small, this is a good time to experiment with mixing tones. The advantage of artist's acrylics is their true, vibrant color. They are easy to paint with and dry quickly when used without a glaze for decorative work. Also, in the long run, they are less expensive because you require only a small amount to be added to a glazing liquid or to commercial paint. Artist's acrylics are not suitable for mixing large quantities of dark color.

GLAZES

Glazing liquid has two important properties that make it an indispensable tool for decorative artists: When mixed with paint it extends the drying time, which allows you to create patterns such as the background drifts in faux marble or to drag a comb or brush through the wet surface. The colored glaze also produces a translucent coating and when applied over a lighter basecoat will appear as several shades of the same color.

Traditionally, only oil-based glazing liquids were available. They were colored with artist's oils and could be used only with oil-based paints. Now, water-based glazing liquids are available to mix with commercial latex paints, water-based craft paints, and artist's acrylics. Colored glazes also come premixed and ready to use in a limited number of colors. Drying times for glaze vary with different manufacturers, so always test before beginning your project.

We have used vinegar to create a glaze for our pioneer Vinegar-Grained Table on pages 70–71. This glaze does not slow down the drying time, but does make the paint colors translucent. This is a historical method of wood-graining, and it must be sealed with several coats of spray varnish. Varnish applied with a brush will remove the finish.

TINTING GLAZE WITH LATEX PAINT

The recipe for a colored or tinted glaze using latex paint varies slightly depending on the project's requirements. A standard combination is 1 part glazing liquid, 1 part paint. For a more translucent coat, add more glazing liquid; for more solid (opaque) coverage, add more paint.

TINTING GLAZE WITH OIL-BASED/ALKYD PAINT

The standard recipe for a tinted glaze using oil-based products is 1 part glazing liquid, 1 part paint, thinned with paint thinner to the consistency of heavy cream.

TINTING GLAZE WITH ARTIST'S ACRYLIC AND ARTIST'S OIL

The general rule is to use 1 teaspoon artist's acrylic or artist's oil to 1 cup of water- or oil-based glazing liquid. The amount you use depends on the translucency or depth required. Mix the artist's paints in small batches using a 1″ artist's brush. Mix very well because the color tends to stay at the bottom of the container.

TINTING GLAZE WITH POWDERED PIGMENTS

Always wear a mask when mixing powders. To color a liter of oil-water-based glaze, use approximately 2 teaspoons of powder. Once again this depends on the depth of color you require. Measure the powder into a small dish and add enough water or enough paint thinner to make a paste. Pour the amount of glaze you require for your project into a clean container and stir in the paste. Mix well.

ANTIQUING THE COLOR OF YOUR PAINT

Add burnt umber to the paint or just apply a tiny amount of artist's acrylic (burnt umber, burnt sienna, or raw sienna) over the dry painted top and wipe it off gently with a clean rag.

PLASTER

Plaster is commonly known as a product to lay over drywall and to fill in cracks. Decorative plasters have recently emerged on the market that contain marble dust and can be polished to varying degrees of sheen. Because of its increased popularity in the decorating market, it's now more readily found in paint stores under a variety of names depending on the manufacturer. These Venetian-type plasters are stunning on walls, but they can also be used in imaginative ways on smaller projects. (See the Plastered Barnwood Shelf on pages 98–99.) Also available are containers of premixed plaster ready to apply for texturing. These do not necessarily have the marble dust added and are used for projects where the sheen from burnishing is not necessary. (I used this type of plaster on the Stone Table on pages 68–69.)

I have only recently begun to use ornamental gesso as a decorative medium. Any artist will tell you that gesso has been around a long time. Painters apply it to canvas to create a very smooth, velvety surface on which to paint. Regular plaster and gesso are meant to be applied in a thin or skim coat. Applied in a thicker layer, it will crack. However, the new ornamental gesso is made with more elasticity and is ideal for raised relief work like stenciling; it also doesn't require any primer. For decorative purposes it is most commonly used to create a raised surface, such as a stenciled border. (See the Bathroom Cabinet Frame on pages 124–25.)

ORNAMENTAL TRIM AND MOLDINGS

There is a tantalizing selection of decorative trim and moldings available at hardware and home decor stores, perfect for adding character to small furnishings and accessories. Generally sold in 8-foot lengths or strips, they come in different widths from ½ inch up to 8 inches and in many designs. You can choose from the very plain cove style, or a lineup of blocks called dentil, so named because it resembles a row of teeth, and other more elaborate cuts such as egg and dart. They are made from wood, MDF, foam, or polyester and are meant to be painted. Also look for other ornamental decorations; carved plaques, medallions, sconces, brackets, and pedestals. These can re-style a shelving unit or dresser quickly and inexpensively, or simply stand alone as a handsome accent piece.

LEAF AND TRANSFERS

Metallic leaf has been used for hundreds of years to gild furnishings and frames. Dutch metal was introduced this century as an inexpensive alternative to the real metals, and is traditionally available in silver, gold, and bronze. The latest evolution is Dutch metal in a variety of metallic colors from cherry red to lime green. Leaf is usually sold in packets of 5-inch squares. It is adhered to the surface with size, a type of sticky varnish. To make gilding easy, dry size is now available in plain or patterned sheets. Once the dry size is transferred onto the surface, sheets of Dutch metal are placed over the top.

For application of silver leaf, see Exotic Canopy on pages 154–55. For colored metallic foil, see Leafed Canvas Floorcloth on pages 168–69.

PAPER

The art of gluing cutout paper to a surface for decoration is called decoupage. It was made wildly popular by the Victorians, who decoupaged everything from walls to furniture and accessories. Today we are seeing an enormous comeback of this decorating style. Decoupaged pieces are popular in upscale decorating stores, and the do-it-yourself market is full of materials and theme kits for creating your own works.

Most types of paper can be cut up and used: wallpaper, wrapping paper, tissue, newspaper, even postcards. There are also decoupage kits filled with motifs ready to cut. The only type of paper to avoid is any coated with plastic, such as vinyl wallcovering. Most popular of all for decoupaging are black-and-white or colored photocopies: They can be sized to fit the designated space, the original paper or photograph is saved, and it's inexpensive to do. Black-and-white copies can be colored by hand with thin washes of acrylic paint, or an aged sepia effect can easily be created by rubbing over the surface with a wet tea bag. Colored photocopies, although once very expensive, are now becoming more affordable.

If you have a lot of cutting to do, invest in a good pair of comfortable, sharp scissors. Small manicure scissors are helpful for cutting around curves, and a craft knife for internal areas.

Types of glue vary with the project. Choose from wallpaper paste, Mod Podge, which is a crafter's mainstay ideal for most projects, white craft glue, or even mucilage (school glue). It's not only the glue that will eventually hold the paper in place, it's the many layers of varnish.

The key to a successful finish is the varnish. Water-based varnish must be used because oil-based varnish would soak into the paper. Water-based varnish goes on milky but dries clear. You should apply at least five coats to fully seal the paper onto the surface and create a smooth surface. Let each coat of varnish dry thoroughly before adding the next.

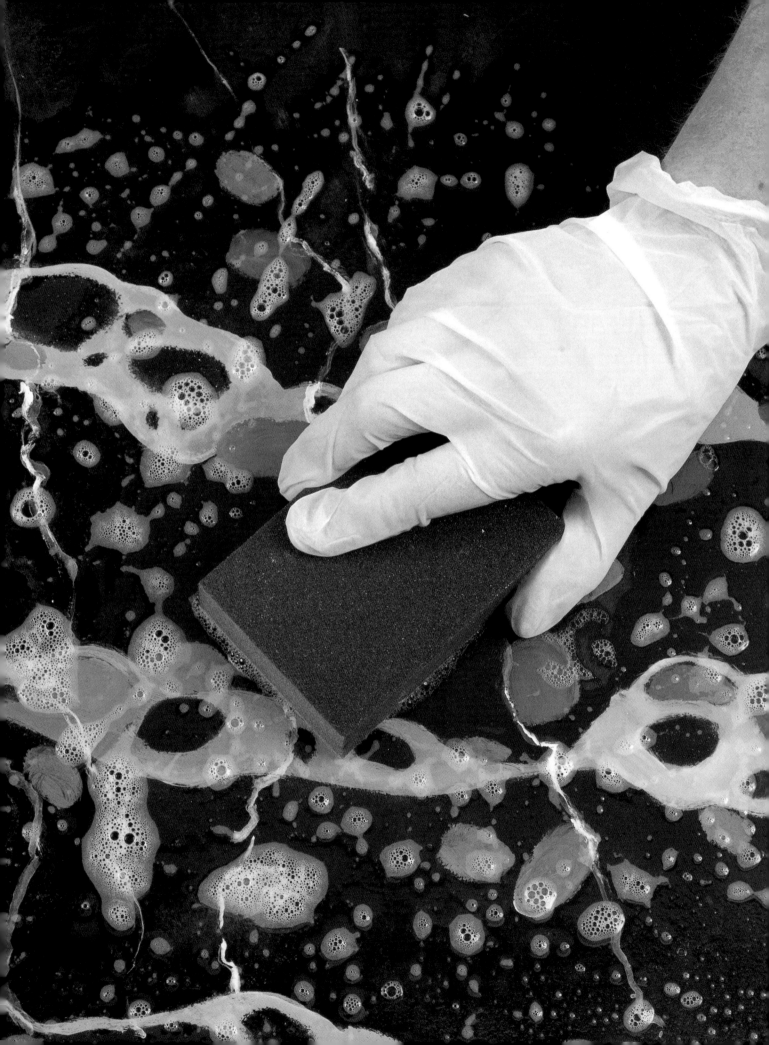

the professional
touch

Furniture restorers and dealers know that the condition of the finished surface of a piece is what gives it the most value. Furniture and home accessories are meant not only to look good, but also to feel good. We are all, at heart, furniture strokers, and put great stock in a silky smooth touch. It's the finish that makes the difference between furniture that you will treasure and something that will soon end up in your yard sale.

It can be heartbreaking to apply coats of varnish to a hand-painted faux marble tabletop that you are immensely proud of, only to have the finishing varnish bumpy to the touch or yellowing within a few days. The following simple but professional tips will ensure your projects look and feel great and remain that way.

PAINT AND GLAZE

The base coat is not the most glamorous step of your painted finish, but it's important because colored glazes are translucent and you can see the base coat through the glaze coat. Any drips or brush marks will show through the glaze.

A base coat is usually two coats, each applied thinly and smoothly. It is even worth sanding the dry first coat lightly before the second coat is applied. Use a tack cloth to remove any dust.

When working with colored glaze, the hallmark of a professional-looking finish is that no one can tell what tool was used. If you are working with a sea sponge, for example, to reproduce the look of stone, blend the pattern so that the edges of the sponge won't be seen. Soften and blend any brush and feather strokes in faux marble, or the illusion will be ruined.

Wet-and-dry sanding ensures a silky smooth finish without scratches. For instructions see page 58.

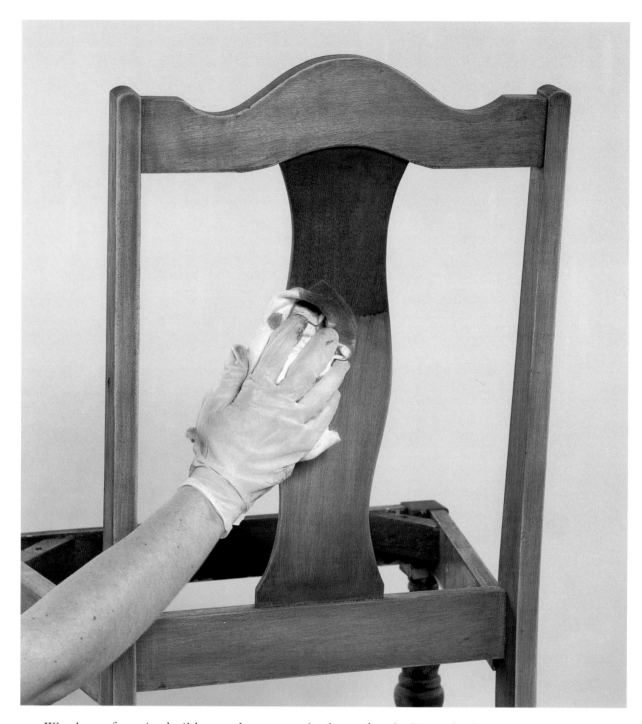

Watch out for paint buildup, and never overload your brush. Dip only the first inch of the brush into the paint or glaze. For more intricate pieces like carved moldings, remove most of the paint from the brush onto a rag or newspaper, and build up the color slowly. Turn your piece around so that you can see the surface from different angles. Apply a thin coat and feather the paint toward the edges and corners. Be careful around the tricky areas such as where a chair leg meets the seat. As much as possible work in natural light. Artificial light creates shadows, which hide defects in the finish that may show up later if you move the piece somewhere else.

STAINS

Stains are less forgiving than paint. A stain is designed to sink into wood and therefore is permanent, whereas paint sits on top of the surface and can be removed or repainted. Because a stain is permanent, it's important to be sure of the color, the depth, and the tool you use to apply it. Test first on a hidden portion of the piece that you are finishing, like underneath the seat of a chair, or inside a dresser drawer. All woods have their own color and will take stain differently.

You can apply stain to wood with a brush or a rag. Always work in the direction of the grain. Apply the stain to a section of two or three square feet and go back over the surface with a rag to remove any excess. As with paint, stain is best applied in thin coats. Once the first coat is dry you may add other thin coats to build up the color; the more coats, the deeper the color, and the less wood grain will be visible

Any piece that has been stained should be sealed with varnish or wax. Once your project has had the decorative effect applied to it, it must be finished to ensure that all your hard work will last for many years and to give the surface a pleasing touch. How you choose to finish your project is as important as the preparation stage. The two most common products for protecting a surface are varnish and wax.

VARNISH

This top, protective coating is marketed under many names—urethane, polyurethane, clear coat, and varnish. For clarity, I have used the term *varnish* throughout the book. As with paint, varnish comes in both water- and oil-based forms. Water-based, acrylic varnishes look milky when applied, but dry clear. Oil-based varnish has a yellowish tint to it, and will yellow even more on the surface over time. Varnish is used for two reasons, to protect your work and to add a particular sheen to the decorative finish. Several coats of varnish will also add depth to a paint finish.

WET-AND-DRY SANDING

This is a method of sanding used by professionals between coats of varnish to create a very smooth finish. It eliminates any small scratches that may result with the dry-sandpaper method and does not create dust. Make a sudsy mixture of soap and water and apply the suds to the surface with a sponge. Sand the surface with fine-grade sandpaper, riding on the suds. Rinse away soap and residue and pat dry with a soft lint-free cloth. For best results, wipe with a tack cloth to ensure that the surface is perfectly clean.

WAX

Several coats of beeswax can be applied over a painted wood project. It is a more authentic finishing method for pieces that have been antiqued. The beeswax should be reapplied and buffed every few months. The buildup of wax will not only add to the authenticity of the piece, but will protect against damage.

Beeswax can also be tinted with black or burnt umber artist's oil to add an aged look to furniture and accessories.

To create a softly textured effect on this Chinese-red painted surface, a little brown paint was added to high-gloss varnish and applied sparingly with a kitchen sponge. Once dry, a coat of clear gloss varnish finished the job.

tips for applying a long-lasting varnish finish

• You **cannot** put water-based varnish over oil-based paint, but you **can** put oil-based varnish over water-based paint.

• To create a glassy smooth finish for a tabletop or chest of drawers, apply the varnish in thin, smooth coats using either a sponge brush or a varnish brush. Neither will leave brush marks.

• Use a tack cloth to remove dust between coats.

• The final coat of varnish should be applied very softly in one direction.

• Varnish is available in several sheens and it is important to use the sheen that relates best to your finish. For example, faux malachite requires a high gloss to look authentic, whereas an antiqued or aged effect should be finished with a matte or low-sheen varnish.

• Spray varnish will give a uniform coating to most surfaces. It is best used for intricate, highly detailed pieces.

• An oil-based spray varnish is required to cover homemade glazes that are water-soluble, such as vinegar graining.

projects
for furnishing your home

tables

Wine crates look as delicious as the product they hold but are free. Here a 1960s box-shaped coffee table was covered with the decorative ends of wine crates. After the crate ends were glued and nailed into place, five coats of high-gloss, oil-based varnish tinted with a small amount of yellow ocher paint was applied, which added a stain plus a deep sheen. A thick length of rope was glued and nailed around the outside edges as a finishing touch. To construct a square table, see the instructions on pages 28–29 for building the Five-Sided Display Box.

Tables have as many personalities as they do uses, and a fresh table finish will add spirit and renewed style to any room. There are countless imaginative treatments waiting to revive a yard-sale find, hand-me-down, or inexpensive purchase. You can also build your own table using two or more different materials. Look for a wrought-iron base, a pair of wooden trestle legs, or even large cement pots—anything that will give solid support for the top. Plywood and MDF can be cut to your specifications for any size and shape, from a tiny round occasional table to an 8-foot-long panel for the dining room. Paint will transform the top into an exotic slab of marble, a cool sheet of steel, or a fine old wood heirloom. If you've never attempted a project before, transforming a tabletop is a great place to start. The flat surface is easy to work on and small enough to make experimentation fun.

1. 2. 3.

farmhouse table

I found this wooden table at a country fair. It was just the right size for a kitchen, and with a little sprucing up I thought it could also do double duty as a garden picnic table in the warm weather. To give it a lighthearted country effect, I painted a white dishtowel over the dark stained wood and to add to the illusion, I let the cloth "drape" over the edge of the table.

MATERIALS AND TOOLS
- low-tack painter's tape
- primer
- white and blue latex paint, satin
- roller and paint tray
- 1" paintbrush
- matte or satin acrylic varnish
- 3" foam brush

INSTRUCTIONS

For the best results, prepare your surface following the guidelines in the preparation section, page 41. After washing and lightly sanding this tabletop, I applied an oak stain over the entire surface.

STEP 1. Mask off a diamond-shaped "cloth" on the tabletop. The effect looks more authentic if the points of the diamond fall over the edges of the table.

STEP 2. Paint the diamond with 1 coat of primer. When dry, apply 2 coats of white paint and let dry for at least 4 hours.

STEP 3. Tape off 2 thin lines around the dishtowel pattern and fill in with the blue paint. Let dry completely.

STEP 4. Apply 2 coats of varnish to the entire table for protection.

rustic provençal
tiled table

I have always adored the tiled kitchen tables found in southern France, and
when a friend asked me to find her one without the expense of buying a
designer piece, I immediately reached for paint. I bought a standard kitchen
table with painted legs and a pine top. I stamped the shapes and colors of
Provençal tiles onto a light gray base coat using pieces cut from kitchen
sponges. The effect is wonderful for any kitchen, especially one with a French
Country theme. For inspiration and ideas for patterns, visit the local library or
the Internet and look under "Mosaics" and/or "French Country Style."

INSTRUCTIONS

For the best results, prepare your surface following the guidelines in the preparation section, page 41. *Note:* When you buy a finished piece of furniture, it's important to rough up the existing varnish with sandpaper before beginning to paint and then apply a coat of high-adhesion primer to ensure durable results. If you are using a regular primer, you should remove all the varnish.

STEP 1. Apply 2 coats of the putty gray base coat and let dry for at least 4 hours.

STEP 2. Design an interesting tile pattern as simple or complex as you wish and draw it lightly onto the tabletop. Cut out tile shapes from kitchen sponges to fit your design: large and small squares, rectangles, and triangles. These tile sponges should be cut a little smaller than their respective table size to leave a "grout" space around each tile impression.

STEP 3. To fill in the design, dampen a sponge tile stamp, dip one end of it into some paint, dab off the excess on a piece of paper towel, and press the sponge onto the surface. The impressions do not have to be perfect as they represent old, worn tiles. Leave about ⅛" space between painted tiles as a grout line. Wash out the sponge before you move on to another color.

STEP 4. When the border is complete, fill in the center of the tabletop using the same sponging technique and a square sponge tile.

STEP 5. Let the table dry for at least 24 hours. Erase pencil marks visible in the grout lines, then apply 2 or 3 coats of matte varnish for protection.

MATERIALS AND TOOLS

BASE COAT
- putty gray latex paint, satin
- 3" foam brush or small roller

PAINTED FINISH
- pencil and ruler
- kitchen sponges
- sharp knife or scissors
- terra-cotta, yellow, and blue latex paint, satin
- paper towels
- matte varnish
- 3" foam brush

stone table

Stone has been used for centuries in Mediterranean kitchens for table and counter tops as well as under foot, as it's an ideal material to help keep the room cool. The tactile textures and neutral colors found in natural stone are once again popular in today's homes. But real stone is expensive, and because of its weight can be impractical. A clever alternative is this contemporary dining table. We already had a stunning wrought-iron base but the top was long gone. A piece of MDF was cut to size and then plastered and painted to look like sandstone. A thin coat of tinted plaster was troweled onto the surface and sponged lightly to reproduce the markings found in stone. Stone colors were then rubbed over the textured dry plaster. To keep the plaster from chipping, the key is three coats of matte varnish, applied once the paint is dry.

MATERIALS AND TOOLS

PLASTER FINISH
- high-adhesion primer
- raw umber and yellow ocher artist's acrylic paint
- 2 cups texture plaster
- mixing containers
- metal spatula
- stir stick
- sea sponge
- water
- fine-grade sandpaper
- water-based glazing liquid
- two 3″ foam brushes
- soft, lint-free rags
- matte varnish

RECIPE
- 1 tablespoon artist's acrylic paint
- 1 cup water-based glazing liquid

excluding the border. Let dry. The reason for not using white primer is when sanding down to the wood you do not want to see any white.

STEP 3. Brush on 1 coat of crackle medium in small patches. Once dry, brush on 1 coat of red paint to the whole area. The cracks will appear only in the areas where there is crackle medium. Let dry completely, about 4 hours.

STEP 4. Sand down random areas of the red coat to expose more of the peach undercoat.

STEP 5. Remove the tape and retape carefully on the other side of the border line.

STEP 6. Apply yellow paint to the border. Let dry. On this table I painted over the large nailheads and sanded them back once the green and yellow coats were dry.

STEP 7. Apply green paint over the yellow border. While the green paint is still tacky, wipe off random patches with a rag, exposing some of the yellow undercoat. Once dry, sand random areas to reveal the wood. Remove the tape and let the paint dry. Wax and buff the surface.

MATERIALS AND TOOLS

PAINTED FINISH
- low-tack painter's tape
- primer
- peach, red, yellow, and green latex paint, matte or satin
- 3″ paintbrushes and/or foam brushes
- crackle medium, available at craft stores
- medium-grade sandpaper
- soft, lint-free rags
- beeswax

faux malachite table

Malachite is one of the richest, most exquisite stones in the world. It has been valued from earliest civilization, and has been used both ground up as a pigment and polished as inlays in furnishings and artifacts. We find pieces of malachite decorating the ornate furniture of Russian czars and the kings and queens of Europe. This ornamental stone is a brilliant blue/green and has a distinctive striped pattern that bends into circles, arcs, and vees when the stone is cut. Lucky for us, the look of malachite is easily reproduced with

MATERIALS AND TOOLS

BASE COAT
- black latex paint, matte or satin
- 3″ foam brush or small roller

PAINTED FINISH
- foam core
- serrated scissors
- low-tack painter's tape
- small roller
- spruce green and forest green latex paint, satin
- water-based glazing liquid
- mixing container
- 3″ foam brush
- badger hair or soft bristle brush
- high-gloss varnish
- 3″ foam brush

RECIPE
- 1 part latex paint
- 1 part water-based glazing liquid

paint. The effect is most successful on small objects or as inlays in furniture, just as the real stone was once used. Its sophisticated color is ideal for elegant pieces such as candlesticks, trinket boxes, or, as I have produced here, a faux inlay around a dining tabletop. This tabletop has been cut from MDF, which provides the necessary smooth base for a faux polished stone finish. The base coat is black. Using silver paint I applied a simple geometric pattern to the center and a border around the edges. Before you begin, study a photograph of a piece of real malachite for reference.

INSTRUCTIONS

For the best results, prepare your surface following the guidelines in the preparation section, page 41. Cut foam-core squares 2″ to 3″ wide, using serrated scissors along one end. This tool is used to create the malachite pattern. They do become soggy with repeated use, so cut 4 or 5 squares.

STEP 1. Apply 2 coats of the black base coat and let dry for 4 hours.

STEP 2. Mask off a 4″ border around the tabletop with low-tack tape, leaving a 1″ border at the edge for silver paint. Using a roller, apply spruce green (the lightest green) paint to the border. Let dry.

STEP 3. Mask off irregular sections around the border in a random pattern of angles to resemble cut pieces of malachite.

STEP 4. Prepare the colored glaze with equal parts dark (forest) green paint and glazing liquid. With a foam brush, apply the glaze to every other masked-off section along the border. Drag the foam-core tool through the wet glaze using a wavy motion to create the patterns found in real malachite. Make each section slightly different.

STEP 5. Hold the badger brush perpendicular to the surface and brush backward and forward very lightly over the glaze to soften and blur the pattern. Let dry completely.

STEP 6. Reverse the tape to protect areas already painted and fill in the remaining border sections. Remove all the tape. Let dry completely.

STEP 7. To finish the tabletop, I painted an accent pattern in the center with silver paint, and filled in the outer 1″ border and edges with silver paint. Apply 3 or 4 coats of high-gloss varnish for sheen and protection.

2.

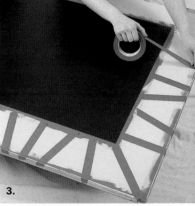

3.

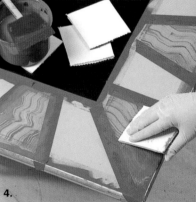

4.

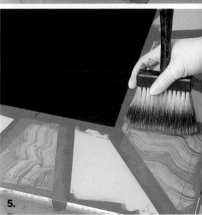

5.

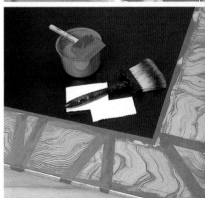

6.

crackle varnish clock table

Crackle varnish has a fascinating history. Furniture manufacturers and art forgers alike have used this sophisticated finishing technique to add years and value to a piece. Two coats of varnish, water- and oil-based, are applied, and because, as we all know, you can't mix oil and water, the varnish actually cracks. Since the varnish is transparent, the cracks are barely visible, but once rubbed with a little raw umber artist's oil, the cracks really stand out, and the entire surface is aged even further by the sepia tone.

This incredible clock table is just a circle of MDF sitting on a square base. The roman numerals and clock hands were stenciled on (the templates are provided on page 187). The hands were given the illusion of standing slightly above the surface by painting in a shadow.

MATERIALS AND TOOLS
• MDF or plywood cut in circle

BASE COAT
• pale cream latex paint, satin
• 3″ paintbrush or foam brush

PAINTED FINISH
• pencil and ruler
• string
• thumbtack
• fine artist's brush
• black latex paint or stencil paint, and dark gray latex paint, satin
• Mylar
• fine indelible black marker
• sharp X-acto knife
• cutting mat
• patterns for clock hands and numerals (templates on page 187)
• stencil brush
• paper towels
• crackle kit
• 2″ foam brush
• burnt umber artist's oil
• soft, lint-free rags
• oil-based varnish
• foam brush

INSTRUCTIONS

For the best results, prepare your surface following the guidelines in the preparation section, page 41. *Note:* If the air is very humid, that will extend the drying time and the varnish won't crack. If you choose to speed up the drying time by using a hair dryer, the cracks will be larger than if your piece dried naturally.

STEP 1. Apply 2 coats of pale cream base coat to the tabletop and let dry for 4 hours.

STEP 2. To find the center of the circle, use a newspaper to trace and cut out a template of the tabletop. Fold the paper circle in half and finger-press to crease the fold. Fold in half again and finger-press to crease. Open the paper circle. The point where the creases intersect is the center. Use the template to mark the center on the tabletop. With a pencil and ruler, draw guidelines and points on the clock

face. You will need 12 equidistant points for the numbers. To mark off a 1″ border for the minutes, tie string to a pencil; measure and cut the string 1″ shorter than the length from the center to the edge of the table (the radius). Secure one end of the string at the center with a thumbtack and draw around the circumference. Cut another 1″ from the string and repeat to draw the inner circle.

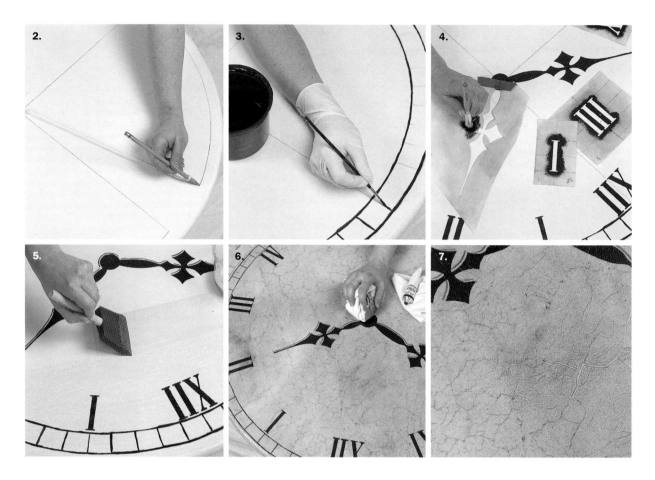

STEP 3. With the fine artist's brush and black paint, paint in the border lines and the minute lines.

STEP 4. With the Mylar, marker, X-acto knife, and cutting mat, make stencils of the minute and hour hands and the numerals from the patterns provided, following the instructions on page 185. Stencil the minute and hour hands and numerals with black paint and a stencil brush. Pour a little black paint on a paint tray. Dip stencil brush into paint. Twirl on paper towel to remove excess paint. Fill in stencil patterns. Let dry completely. Apply a hand-painted line in dark gray above the hands as a shadow.

STEP 5. Apply the crackle coats to the tabletop following the manufacturer's instructions. This is available in kit form. Do not use commercial water-based and oil-based varnish together.

STEP 6. Squeeze a little burnt umber artist's oil onto a rag and rub the color over the surface to highlight the cracks.

STEP 7. Protect your surface with 2 coats of oil-based varnish.

Whereas the Crackle Varnish Clock Table is crackled varnish, this coffee table is crackled paint. Originally a heavy-looking oak stained table, we lightened it up with taupe and white paint; the taupe served as the basecoat. Then a layer of crackle medium was applied and let dry. Finally, the white topcoat was brushed on, and as the paint dried, the cracks appeared, the color of the taupe basecoat.

crackle paint coffee table

MATERIALS AND TOOLS

BASE COAT
- black latex paint, any sheen
- small roller or foam brush

PAINTED FINISH
- white candle
- red latex paint, any sheen
- small roller or foam brush
- fine steel wool
- high-gloss oil-based varnish
- foam brush

Negoro Nuri is a fourteenth-century Japanese lacquer finish that is still used to decorate display dishes. True Japanese lacquer is a refined and lustrous finish, but by using the traditional black and red colors and a couple of layers of high-gloss varnish it is easy to create an easy westernized version of this stunning effect. Here I applied Negoro Nuri to the top of a low Japanese-style table bought from a futon shop, but it could also be used on trays, lamp bases, or delicate objects with equal success. Candle wax is rubbed in patches between layers of black and red paint. The red is rubbed back lightly to reveal some of the black base coat. Left at this stage, the flat paint would look antiqued, but when high-gloss varnish is applied to the top, depth is created along with the sheen reminiscent of Japanese lacquer.

INSTRUCTIONS

For the best results, prepare your surface following the guidelines in the preparation section, page 41.

STEP 1. Apply 2 coats of black base coat and let dry for 4 hours.

STEP 2. Rub the candle randomly over the surface, leaving patches of wax.

STEP 3. Apply 2 coats of red paint to cover the surface completely. Let dry.

STEP 4. Burnish the entire surface by rubbing it lightly with steel wool. Red paint will come away from the areas that have candle wax underneath.

STEP 5. Make sure all the candle wax is rubbed off and then apply 2 coats of high-gloss oil-based varnish.

japanese lacquer table

storage

Storage containers come in many shapes and sizes, and as well as serving a practical purpose, they offer a perfect opportunity for decoration. There never seem to be enough places to put things away, but often from this challenge come the most imaginative solutions. Antique and modern reproductions of armoires have become a favorite choice for housing everything from home entertainment systems to folded bath and bed linens, toys, and books. We all need a chest of drawers somewhere in the house, and unless you are willing to spend a great deal for fine cabinetry, your options are probably limited to a very plain design. The inexpensive models, however, provide a perfect flat surface for paint and decoration. We can never do without shelving, but it doesn't have to be your standard white laminate, although even these can be reinvented. Be as creative with the actual shelves as with the objects that sit on them. Decorative brackets are available in a variety of different shapes and sizes, from wrought iron, plaster, wood, and Styrofoam to cement and plastic, all of which can be painted. Treat the shelves to adventurous colors and finishes to coordinate with the character of your room.

Traditionally, antique pine armoires are painted in muted heritage colors to fit the era, but with this armoire I have broken every rule, showing off vibrant blues, reds, and greens. I applied two different techniques to replicate an aged and weathered surface: crackle and antiquing, with layers of paint rubbed down and sanded in areas back to the wood.

toile dresser

This handsome dresser was originally found in a yard sale. Although it was covered in unattractive peeling green paint, the drawers all worked smoothly and the wood itself was in great shape. I stripped, sanded, and primed the piece, then applied a colorwash of yellow ocher glaze for age and texture. The French

2.

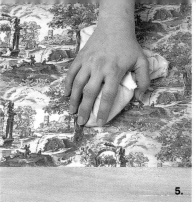

4.

5.

6.

MATERIALS AND TOOLS

BASE COAT
- cream latex paint, satin
- 3″ foam brush or small roller

PAINTED FINISH
- yellow ocher latex paint, satin, or artist's acrylic
- water-based glazing liquid
- mixing container
- soft, lint-free rags

DECOUPAGE
- toile-printed wrapping paper (or wallpaper)
- iron (optional)
- scissors
- pencil and ruler
- wallpaper paste
- 2″ paintbrush
- soft, lint-free rags
- water-based varnish
- foam brush
- upholstery studs (available by the roll)
- hammer

RECIPE
- 1 part latex paint
- 1 part water-based glazing liquid

Country detail for the dresser was added when I discovered wrapping paper with a beautiful toile design, more typically seen on wallpapers and fabric. Toile de Jouy is a French print depicting pastoral scenes of life from a bygone age. The finishing touch was a border design of upholstery studs, which are available by the roll. They are held in place by a handful of individual studs.

INSTRUCTIONS

For the best results, prepare your surface following the guidelines in the preparation section, page 41. Also see Preparing Wood Furniture for Paint, page 47.

STEP 1. Apply 2 coats of cream base coat and let dry for 4 hours.

STEP 2. Mix the yellow ocher glaze. Rub the colored glaze over the surface with a rag. Use long strokes and move in one direction creating a simple wood grain. Let the glaze dry from 4 to 12 hours.

STEP 3. If it is creased, iron the toile wrapping paper smooth, using a low heat setting. Lay the paper in position, centered on the dresser top. If necessary, cut paper to desired size. Once it is in the correct place, mark guidelines with a pencil and ruler.

STEP 4. Brush wallpaper paste onto the back of the paper and reposition the paper on the top of the dresser using the guidelines to ensure that it is straight. Use a clean rag to smooth out any bubbles or raised areas.

STEP 5. To give the paper an aged appearance that complements the base, rub a little of the ocher glaze over it using a rag. When completely dry, apply 3 coats of varnish to the entire dresser top.

STEP 6. Mark out a diamond pattern on the paper. Hammer a string of upholstery studs along the edges of the paper and over the diamond pattern lines.

magnificent marble

Techniques for using paints and glazes to simulate the patterns found in real marble have been employed for centuries, either to create an inexpensive substitute or to use in places for which the real stone was far too heavy. There are as many methods and paint recipes as there are varieties of marble. The marble I reproduced on the top of this dresser is called *Portoro,* a black-and-gold marble. It is one of the most exquisite stones in the world, but the mine in Italy that originally produced it is now empty, so it has become quite rare. To complement the marble top, I ragged the drawers with pistachio green paint. A dresser of this standing deserved a set of new handles, and with that, a scruffy garage sale find became something quite special.

MATERIALS AND TOOLS

BASE COAT
- black latex paint, satin
- 3″ paintbrush or foam brush

PAINTED FINISH
- light gray, medium gray, raw sienna, burnt sienna, burnt umber, yellow ocher, and white artist's acrylic paints
- water-based glazing liquid
- mixing containers
- soft, lint-free rags
- artist's brush or small brush
- script liner (very fine artist's brush)
- high-gloss oil-based varnish
- foam brush

RECIPE
- 1 tablespoon artist's acrylic paint
- ½ cup water-based glazing liquid

INSTRUCTIONS

For the best results, prepare your surface following the guidelines in the preparation section, page 41. Also see Preparing Wood Furniture for Paint, page 47.

STEP 1. Apply 2 coats of black base coat and let dry for 4 hours.

STEP 2. Mix a colored glaze using the light gray artist's acrylic. Use a rag and wash the glaze over the entire surface to soften and break up the black base coat. Let dry.

STEP 3. Mix a small amount of raw sienna, burnt sienna, burnt umber, and yellow ocher with a small brush to create an earthy yellow brown. Add a bit of white to tone it down. Add a little glazing liquid to make the paint easier to move.

STEP 4. Paint bands of wavy horizontal lines that look like a series of irregularly shaped bubbles, swelling and then slimming down to a thin line.

STEP 5. With a clean rag, lightly wipe off different-shaped bubbles within the larger bubbles. If the paint has started to dry, dampen the rag with water.

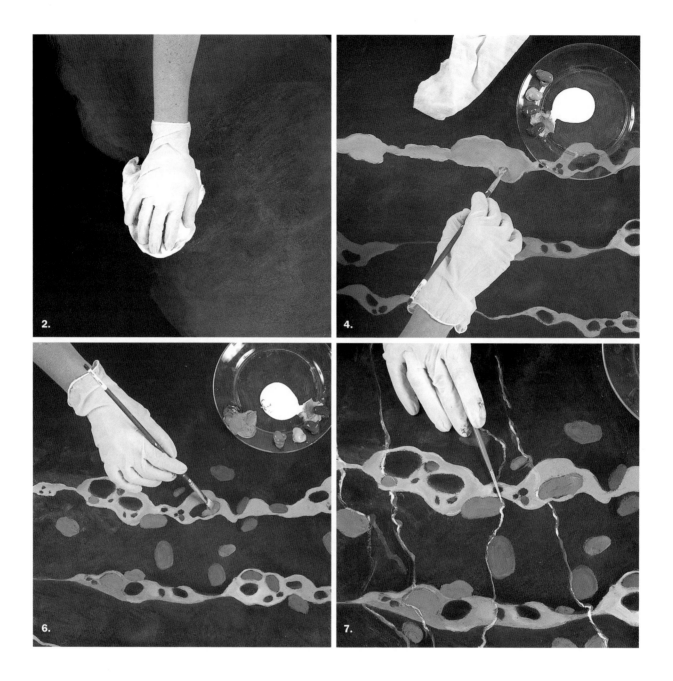

STEP 6. Dip an artist's brush into medium gray paint and draw ellipses over the surface. Vary the size and fill in some of the black bubbles.

STEP 7. Use a script liner or a fine artist's brush to paint white veins perpendicular to the bubbles. Avoid curves or zigzags. Create a rolling flow by holding your brush with your palm facing up and rolling the brush over the surface in one continuous motion. Let dry.

STEP 8. Apply 3 coats of high-gloss oil-based varnish to give the marble added depth and to protect the surface.

georgian display

The Georgians loved moldings and details in their homes. They used plaster moldings and sconces on walls, ceilings, and fireplaces. Inspired by these ornate homes, I added elegant homemade shelving to the walls of a sophisticated study. Pieces of MDF were decorated with stock trim and given a rich ebony effect. Borrowing an idea from the classic finishing touch on fine furniture, I hammered bronze upholstery tacks along the edge of the boards. The shelves sit on plaster sconces given an antique finish. The finished project is an impressive display with Georgian flair.

shelf

MATERIALS AND TOOLS

- ½″ MDF, measured and cut to size (our shelves are 12″ deep and of various lengths from 18″ to 5′)
- dentil molding, the length and twice the depth of the shelf
- water-based primer
- black latex paint, satin
- 3″ paintbrush
- brown water-based stain
- soft, lint-free rags
- finishing nails
- hammer
- brass upholstery studs

INSTRUCTIONS

STEP 1. Prime the shelf and moldings and then apply 2 coats of black base coat. Let dry.

STEP 2. Dip the paintbrush into the brown stain. Remove the excess onto a rag, then dry-brush the shelf, lightly skimming the top of the board.

STEP 3. Repeat step 2 on the molding.

STEP 4. Attach the molding to the shelf with finishing nails, making sure each nail is slightly off-center on the dentil.

STEP 5. Hammer upholstery studs into the center of each dentil, covering the finishing nails with the head of the stud.

sconces

MATERIALS AND TOOLS

- decorative plaster or plastic sconces
- primer
- pale green, bronze, burnt sienna, and ocher latex paint, satin
- 1″ paintbrushes
- soft, lint-free rag
- stencil brush

INSTRUCTIONS

For best results, prepare your surface following the guidelines in the preparation section, page 41.

STEP 1. Prime the sconces and let dry.

STEP 2. Apply 2 coats of the pale green paint, making certain you get into all the crevices. Let dry.

STEP 3. Apply 1 thin coat of bronze paint, letting a small amount of the green base coat show through in spots. Let dry.

STEP 4. Apply the burnt sienna loosely over the sconces. Rub lightly with a soft rag to let the bronze show through. Let dry.

STEP 5. With a stencil brush, dab on ocher paint to highlight the points with the highest relief. Let dry.

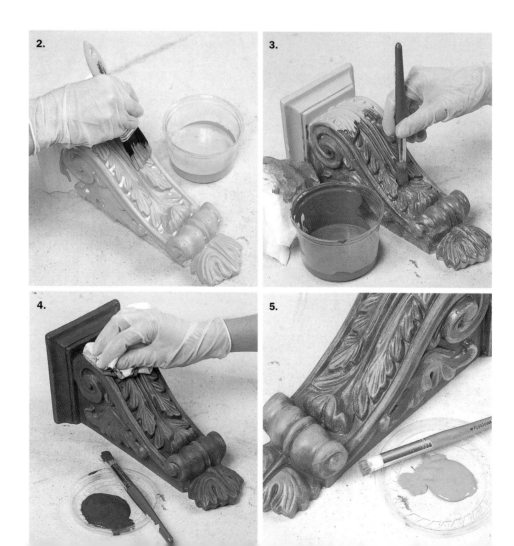

scandinavian
chest of drawers

Inspired by Swedish art, I decorated a plain pine chest of drawers with the soft, mellow colors indigenous of Scandinavian style. If the thought of hand-painting designs fills you with fear, then decoupage is your best friend. It is difficult to tell that the detail on these drawers is only cut wrapping paper. The trick is to sand down the edges of the paper so they blend into the surface. Under many coats of varnish this wouldn't be necessary, but on a piece of furniture you will be applying only one or two coats. A gentle piece like this is perfect for a guest bedroom or even a young girl's room.

MATERIALS AND TOOLS

- ½" and ¼" low-tack painter's tape
- olive green, gray, and white latex paint, satin
- water-based glazing liquid
- mixing container
- paintbrushes
- rags
- color photocopies of designs to fit behind and around handles
- scissors or utility knife
- fine-grade sandpaper
- wallpaper paste or white craft glue
- satin acrylic varnish
- foam brush

RECIPE

- add a little white paint to gray to lighten it, then
- 1 part latex paint
- 1 part water-based glazing liquid

INSTRUCTIONS

For the best results, prepare your surface following the guidelines in the preparation section, page 41. Also see Preparing Wood Furniture for Paint, page 47.

Note: When you buy a finished piece of furniture, it's important to rough up the existing varnish with sandpaper before beginning to paint and then apply a coat of high-adhesion primer to ensure durable results. If you are using a regular primer, you should remove all the varnish.

STEP 1. Remove the drawer handles. Measure and mask off an insert panel with ½″ low-tack tape on the front of the drawers.

STEP 2. Apply 2 coats of olive green base coat to the dresser except for the taped-off areas. Let dry for 4 hours.

STEP 3. Remove the tape and retape on the outside edge of the white panels. Paint the inside of the panels gray. Remove the tape and let dry.

STEP 4. Apply ¼″ tape over the gray color around the frame of the drawers.

STEP 5. Mix the light gray glaze. Dip a paintbrush into the colored glaze, take off the excess on a rag, and apply with a dry brush to the entire dresser. Work in one direction holding the brush perpendicular to the surface. This produces a soft, grainy quality. Let dry; remove the tape. You are left with a muted green chest, muted gray panels, and a solid gray border around the panels.

STEP 6. Cut out the color photocopies to cover the area behind the handles. Sand the edges of the paper gently by moving the sandpaper from the middle of the paper out, so the edges blend into the surfaces. Apply glue to the image and secure it in place. I also glued the paper to the front of the drawer pulls.

STEP 7. Apply 2 coats of varnish for protection. Reattach the drawer pulls.

houndstooth
steamer trunk

Spend a few hours in a fabric store and you will discover an abundance of glorious patterns. Today, some of the fine materials seen traditionally only in men's high-quality clothing stores have become fashionable not only for women's wear but also for home furnishings. The look of flannel, pinstripe, and my favorite, houndstooth, can all be reproduced with paint. I discovered this old wooden trunk at a flea market. Its unadorned surface was perfect for the houndstooth design. I took a piece of fabric, blew it up on a photocopier, and cut out a stencil. It's easier to work with a geometric stencil on a flat surface because it is difficult to move around curves. As a finishing touch, I added an oversized keyhole that suits the original brass handles. This superb storage piece now looks better than it was ever meant to be and makes a grand addition to a study or masculine bedroom.

INSTRUCTIONS

For the best results, prepare your surface following the guidelines in the preparation section, page 41.

STEP 1. Apply 2 coats of tan base coat and let dry for 4 hours. With the Mylar, marker, X-acto knife, and cutting mat, make a stencil of the houndstooth pattern provided, following the instructions on pages 184–86.

STEP 2. Tape off a border. Mark out where the stencil will repeat and

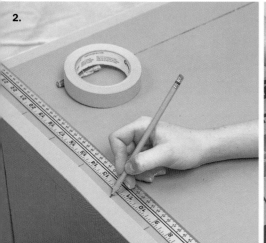

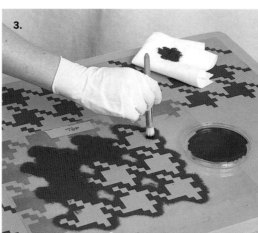

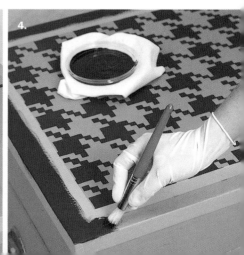

work out how many will fit inside the border. Adjust the border accordingly if necessary. Spray the back of the stencil with adhesive.

STEP 3. Using a stencil brush, fill in the houndstooth stencil with black paint. Let dry.

STEP 4. Once dry, reverse the tape and paint border. (The border is painted in last so that you can adjust it to match up perfectly next to the stencil.)

STEP 5. I hand-painted an old-fashioned keyhole around the original hole with bronze paint.

shabby chic bookcases

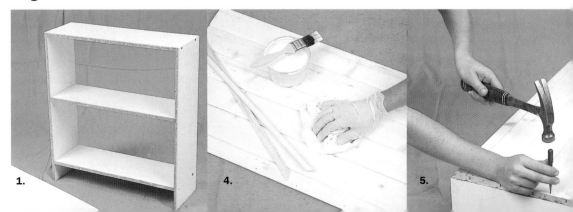

1.

4.

5.

MATERIALS AND TOOLS

- white laminate shelving unit
- wainscoting to fit the back of the shelving unit
- ½" trim molding (to cover the front edges)
- decorative wood shelf the same size or slightly larger than the top of the unit
- handsaw
- miter box (optional)
- medium-grade sandpaper
- oil-based primer
- pale pink latex paint, satin
- water-based glazing liquid
- mixing container
- soft, lint-free rags
- 1" and ¾" finishing nails
- hammer
- nail set
- wood filler
- small spatula
- fine-grit sanding sponge
- paint roller and tray
- 1" paintbrush

RECIPE

- 1 part latex paint
- 1 part water-based glazing liquid

At some time or other we have all bought a set of laminate bookshelves as a temporary storage solution, fully intending to replace them later with something more decorative. However, somehow they seem to hang around forever, occasionally banished to the basement or a child's room. Although functional, they are plain and boring. But with some paint, wainscoting, and trim I gave this set of laminate shelves a shabby-chic makeover.

INSTRUCTIONS

STEP 1. Remove the back from the laminate shelves.

STEP 2. Measure and cut the wainscoting to fit the back of the shelving unit. Cut trim molding to fit the front and side edges of the shelves, mitering the corners (see page 31).

STEP 3. Cut the wood shelf to the right length for the top of the unit. Sand the edges to round them. Prime the board; do not prime the wainscoting or trim molding.

STEP 4. Mix the pale pink glaze. Wash the glaze over the top of the wainscoting and the trim molding with a rag. Let dry.

STEP 5. Attach the wainscoting to the back of the shelving unit, nailing each board in separately at the bottom and the top. Countersink the nailheads with the nail set.

STEP 6. Attach the shelf to the top with 1 nail in each corner. Countersink the nailheads.

STEP 7. Fill the nail holes with wood filler. Let dry, sand smooth, and touch up with primer and paint.

STEP 8. Apply 2 base coats of pale pink latex to the wooden top.

STEP 9. Nail the trim molding to the side and front edges. Countersink the nailheads. Fill the nail holes and touch up with primer and pink glaze. Let dry.

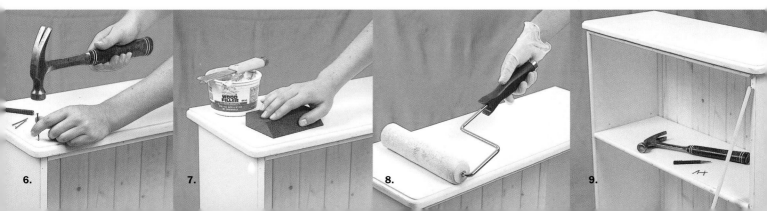

6.   7.   8.   9.

plastered
barnwood shelf

There is something very beautiful about the rough shapes of old barnwood. I wanted to add color and exaggerate the texture of an old plank I had found. Instead of paint, I applied a base coat of pale blue Venetian plaster and then smoothed a vibrant cobalt blue plaster over the top with a metal spatula. The layers of brightly colored plaster work brilliantly with the rough texture of the wood. The ornamental cement brackets and the barnwood shelves are unusual partners, but they complement each other perfectly.

MATERIALS AND TOOLS
- old barnwood board
- wire brush
- medium-grade sandpaper
- water-based varnish
- foam brush
- light and dark blue Venetian plaster
- 3″ paintbrush
- metal spatula
- wall brackets and screws

INSTRUCTIONS

STEP 1. To remove dirt and any flaking paint, scrub the barnwood with a wire brush and a little soapy water. Don't soak the board because old barnwood is very porous and will take a long time to dry out. Sand any very rough spots.

STEP 2. To seal the board, apply water-based varnish to both sides and the edges.

STEP 3. Using a paintbrush, apply 1 coat of the light blue plaster, making sure to get the plaster into all the grooves and indentations of the wood.

1.

2.
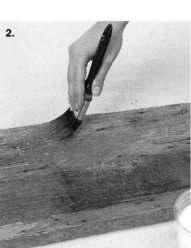

3.

4.

STEP 4. With the metal spatula, apply the second plaster color immediately, pulling a thin coat along the top of the board. Allow the lighter color to show through. The thinner the plaster, the faster it will dry. As it dries, burnish it with the spatula. Leave some areas flat and make others shiny. This burnishing technique will work only with Venetian plaster, as it has marble dust in it.

STEP 5. Attach the brackets to the wall and place the board on top.

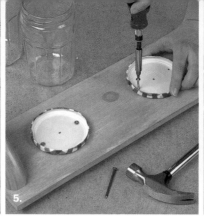

jam jar storage shelf

This dual-purpose shelf is based on a similar construction I first saw in my grandfather's toolshed. He used his jars for screws, nails, and widgets. But the idea is so simple, I thought it would be a practical idea for a tiny kitchen. Any glass jars can be used; look for large ones with interesting metal lids, and make sure the lids screw on securely.

MATERIALS AND TOOLS

- small amount of orange and rose latex paint, satin
- water-based glazing liquid
- mixing containers
- ready-cut shelf
- soft, lint-free rags
- shelf brackets
- acrylic semigloss varnish
- 2″ foam brush
- empty glass jars with screw-on lids
- pencil and ruler
- nail
- hammer
- screws slightly shorter than the thickness of the shelf
- screwdriver

RECIPE

- 1 part latex paint
- 1 part water-based glazing liquid

INSTRUCTIONS

For best results, prepare your surface following the guidelines in the preparation section, page 41.

STEP 1. Mix the orange and rose glazes.

STEP 2. Apply the glazes lightly over the surfaces of the shelf and brackets with a rag, wiping in the direction of the wood grain. Both colors can be applied at the same time to create a subtle streaking. Let dry.

STEP 3. Apply 2 coats of varnish for protection. Let dry.

STEP 4. On the underside of the shelf, with a pencil and ruler, mark the jar lid positions so that each one is evenly placed.

STEP 5. Puncture 2 holes in each lid with a hammer and nail, then secure the lids to the underside of the shelf with screws. (Make sure the screws don't break through the top of the shelf.)

STEP 6. Attach the brackets to the shelf and the unit to the wall. Screw the jars in to their lids.

1.   2.   3.   4.

When an Indian friend asked me for ideas on how to display a collection of artifacts from her homeland, I took my inspiration from the local embossed silver patterns that are popular in India on so many home accessories. I found a series of black wooden boxes at a garage sale. One side of each cube was open so that small brackets could be attached on the inside, allowing the boxes to sit flush against the wall. You can build similar boxes yourself (see pages 28–29 for instructions). To replicate the intricate silver patterns, I attached paper and string to the surface to create a design in relief. I covered them with aluminum foil, then tarnished them with black paint.

MATERIALS AND TOOLS
- wood boxes (to build your own, see instructions on pages 28–29)
- pencil and ruler
- cardboard, string, or other material that will make a relief pattern
- scissors
- aluminum foil
- carpenter's glue
- black commercial or artist's acrylic paint
- soft, lint-free rag and cloth
- brackets and hooks for hanging

INSTRUCTIONS

STEP 1. Draw a pattern directly onto the box with a pencil and ruler.

STEP 2. Cut cardboard shapes and pieces of string and glue them into position on the box to fill in the pattern that you have drawn. This creates a raised design on the flat surface. Do not put a raised design on the top of the box; leave it flat as you will be setting things on it. Let dry thoroughly.

STEP 3. Cut a piece of aluminum foil larger than your surface. Working on one side at a time, apply glue over the complete design surface including the wood, cardboard, and string. Lay down the foil, either side up, smoothing it and pushing it into the relief grooves with your fingers. Let dry. Cut off the excess foil. Repeat for the other box sides.

STEP 4. Using a rag, rub all five sides lightly with black acrylic paint, leaving more paint behind in the grooves of the design. Use a soft cloth to buff and highlight the relief.

STEP 5. Attach brackets and hang as shown in the instructions on pages 28 and 29.

bombay boxes

screens

Screens were very popular in the Victorian era. They were used as functional decoration, to divide a room, block a window, or offer privacy for dressing. Screens are once again back in fashion, and we use them much the same way today. These versatile performers can hide a mess or organize everything from postcards and letters to pots and pans. They are easy to make in any shape or size, and decorating a screen is as simple as applying a couple of coats of a glorious color or creating a unique effect with shredded paper and gingko leaves. Because it may be difficult to find a ready-made screen that is the right size for your needs, we've given complete instructions for building your own on page 27.

Building a screen can be as simple as hinging together flat wood panels and applying a few coats of paint. This chartreuse green screen makes a bold statement standing in a room with black walls and collectible art.

tropical screen

Painting a screen is similar to painting a canvas; it is a purely personal experience. The results can be as artistic or as basic as you desire. If freehand painting frightens you, keep the design simple. The inspiration for this screen came from a Caribbean holiday I took with my family. A naive tree was painted with light brushstrokes over each pastel panel. This beautiful serene picture suits a feminine bedroom or sitting room. I attached cork board to the back of the screen for pinning up photographs and notes, but you could just simply paint the back.

MATERIALS AND TOOLS
- screen panels (to build your own, see instructions on page 27)

BASE COAT
- light cream latex paint, satin
- 3" paintbrush

PAINTED FINISH
- low-tack painter's tape
- burnt orange latex, satin
- water-based glazing liquid
- mixing container
- foam brush
- photocopy of chosen design
- carbon paper
- pencil
- artist's acrylic paints for your design, light brown artist's acrylic
- artist's brush
- hinges and screws

RECIPE
- 1 part latex paint
- 1 part water-based glazing liquid

106

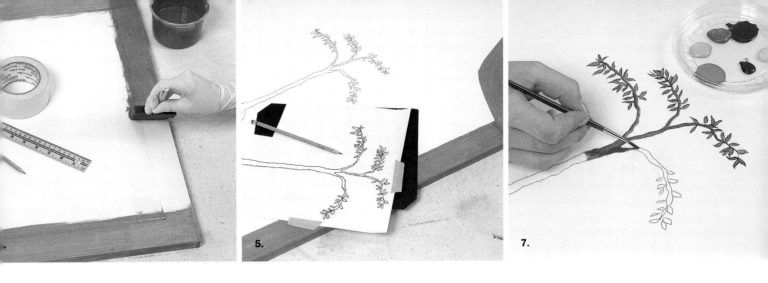

5.

7.

INSTRUCTIONS

STEP 1. Apply 2 coats of light cream base coat to the panels. Let dry for 4 hours.

STEP 2. Measure and tape off a border around the screen. Cut small pieces of tape to work around the curved lines.

STEP 3. Mix the orange glaze. To create a strié border, apply the colored glaze with a foam brush, first along the horizontal, then the vertical, and finally the curved top. Then pull the same foam brush straight through the wet glaze, producing fine lines. Remove the tape and allow 4 hours for the border to dry.

STEP 4. If you feel you can't hand-paint a design, photocopy an image you want and enlarge it to the right size for your screen.

STEP 5. Mark where the design is going to be. Tape a piece of carbon paper over the position and tape the photocopied image over the carbon paper.

STEP 6. With a pencil, trace over the photocopy to transfer the design to the surface of the panel (see instructions on pages 184–85).

STEP 7. Use artist's acrylics mixed with a bit of glaze so the paint will glide on the surface of the panel. Paint in the design using an artist's brush.

STEP 8. To add a shadow line around the border, tape off ¼″ of the cream base coat along the top and one side of each border. Fill in the space with light brown acrylic paint. This will give you the illusion that the border is slightly raised.

STEP 9. Join the panels with door hinges.

wire hangup

Chicken wire is the best solution for anyone who is short on kitchen cupboard space. But whoever thought it could look stylish! All you need is a wooden frame on which to attach the chicken wire so you have a taut strong mesh. This frame can be fixed to a wall or can be used as a screen. A freestanding screen will hold a reasonable number of kitchen objects. Just make sure that the three panels are positioned for good balance.

INSTRUCTIONS

See page 27 for instructions on how to make a basic screen frame.

STEP 1. Cut chicken wire to size slightly smaller than the outside measurements of the frame.

STEP 2. Staple the wire to the frame with the staple gun.

STEP 3. Nail strips of trim over the raw edges of the wire with finishing nails. Simple S-hooks, available at any hardware store, can be used to hang a variety of kitchen utensils.

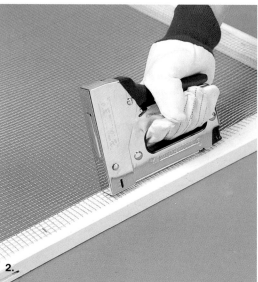

1.

2.

3.

classical screen

MATERIALS AND TOOLS

- black latex paint, satin
- template material (cardboard or fiberboard)
- pencil and ruler
- metallic gold spray paint
- photocopied design
- scissors
- decoupage glue
- high-gloss water-based varnish
- foam brush
- fine-grade sandpaper

Although screens have so many uses, they can also play the role of a movable piece of art. This stunning example was made by a friend of mine who is a professional decoupeur. She used photocopies from a calendar of ancient urns that were glued onto panels of MDF. Five coats of high-gloss varnish provide a silky-smooth shine. This lacquered finish is achieved by allowing each coat of varnish to dry completely, and then wet-and-dry sanding and removing any dust with a tack cloth between coats.

INSTRUCTIONS

To make your own screen see the instructions on page 27.

STEP 1. Apply 2 coats of black base coat to the panels and let dry for 4 hours. Make a template for the inset panels from cardboard or fiberboard. Here I've used fiberboard and attached two pieces of wood to the back to help lift the template without smudging. This stage can be done with masking tape, but as we are working on four separate screen panels, a template is much faster. Make the template 1″ smaller than the panel all around to leave space for the borders.

STEP 2. Position the template on the panel and spray the inset area and the edges with gold paint, creating a mottled metallic effect. Lift the template off the panel carefully. You now have 3 metallic inset panels per screen panel and a one-inch border around each screen. Let dry.

STEP 3. Photocopy your chosen image to size and cut out. These are color copies of antique urns.

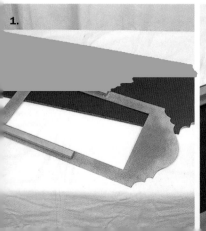

1.

2.

3.

4.

STEP 4. Glue an image into the center of each inset panel. Let dry.

STEP 5. Apply 4 coats of high-gloss varnish. It's important to use water-based varnish. Use the wet-and-dry sanding method for a smooth, professional finish (see finishing information pages 57–58).

rice-paper collage

Collage is the artistic technique of building a pattern of overlapping pieces of paper, material, or any object that can be adhered to a surface. I made a paper collage on this screen with a natural theme using gingko leaves and different papers. Sheets of watercolor paper were attached to the screen's wood frame with a staple gun. Watercolor paper must be used as it absorbs water and then will shrink back taut, whereas other papers will bubble and warp. Then, different shapes cut from natural Japanese rice paper (often used as wrapping paper)

and a collection of gingko leaves were adhered to the damp paper with water-based varnish. A final coating of tissue paper was layered over the surface, again adhered with layers of varnish. Working with damp papers and varnish makes the screen become tighter and tighter, just like a drum. What's beautiful about this natural-looking screen is that it's not only a room divider, but it's also a transparent piece of art that changes with the different light in the room.

INSTRUCTIONS

Note: You must use water-based varnish.

STEP 1. Prime the frames and apply 2 coats of the cream semi-gloss base coat.

STEP 2. Soak the watercolor paper in water until it is saturated. Lay individual sheets onto the frame smoothly and staple down. As the paper dries, it will tighten up. Continue to add sheets to the frame overlapping about ½″ until the framed space is covered.

STEP 3. Dampen and then arrange your bits of artistic paper and leaves on top of the wet paper in any pattern you choose.

STEP 4. Varnish over the watercolor paper and under and over the pieces you have arranged while the paper is still wet. The varnish acts as an adhesive. Varnish between the overlapping seams as well.

STEP 5. Lay sheets of tissue paper over the screen, overlapping to fill in the entire area of the screen. Varnish a thin layer over the top. Tear off any excess that goes past the edge of the frame.

STEP 6. Tear 1″ strips of the brown paper and the rice paper and soak them in water. Apply varnish around the edges of the screen and press the torn strips down to hide the staples. Varnish again over the top of the strips.

STEP 7. While the paper is still wet, turn the screen on its side and varnish the back side of the watercolor paper. When all the paper dries out it will be as a taut as a drum with the paper and leaves neatly sealed as if floating.

frames
and mirrors

Framed pictures and mirrors play an important role in decoration. Adding creative flair to the frames will enhance your photographs, pictures, and mirrors. These are the special touches that personalize your home, and make treasured gifts as well.

Professional framers offer an endless variety of styles and settings for your photography and art, but they are costly. Ready-made frames come with less detail and limited sizes, but they can be decorated with any type of finish to coordinate with your artwork. You can also make your own frame, either cut from MDF or a variety of moldings. Or frames can be painted directly onto the wall. Interesting frames will enhance the most ordinary picture or mirror, and you can even decorate the mirror itself.

Squares of silver and gold leaf were applied in a geometric pattern on a frame built from stock moldings.

etched-glass mirror

A piece of etched glass or mirror has several uses. Etching a pattern on a window is not only decorative, it will allow a degree of privacy; an old glass tabletop can be given a completely new style; and an inexpensive piece of mirror can become a work of art. Remember, though, that whatever project you etch, the finish is permanent. The etching solution used actually eats into the top layer of the glass, producing a matte effect in the shape of your design. Stencils can be used to create a specific pattern, but they must be pressed into place well so that none of the etching solution leaks underneath. I decorated this mirror by cutting curlicues into a sheet of self-adhesive Con-Tact paper that I first pressed onto the mirror. The sticky Con-Tact paper adheres better than a stencil and prevents leaks. As a finishing touch I attached bulldog clips to the frame with pins for hanging invitations, photographs, and other paraphernalia.

MATERIALS AND TOOLS
- picture frame (to build your own, see instructions on pages 30–31)
- mirror cut to fit frame
- self-adhesive shelf paper such as Con-Tact paper
- marker
- sharp X-acto knife
- damp cloth
- glass etching cream, available at craft stores
- artist's brush
- rubber gloves
- mask
- glass cleaner
- paper towels

INSTRUCTIONS

STEP 1. Cover the mirror with Con-Tact paper, smoothing out any bubbles as you roll it on. Con-Tact paper sticks firmly to glass so no etching cream can leak underneath, ensuring a sharp image.

STEP 2. With a marker, draw random curlicues in varying sizes directly onto the Con-Tact paper. Cut out the shapes with the X-acto knife and peel off the paper cutouts. Rub the surface with a damp cloth to remove any remaining adhesive in the open spaces.

STEP 3. Brush a thick coat of the glass etching cream over the cut-away curlicues. Be sure to wear gloves and a mask, as the cream is quite toxic. Let

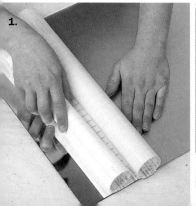
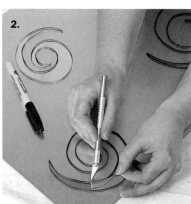

the cream set for 5 minutes and then rinse it off thoroughly with warm water. The curlicues will now be dull.

STEP 4. Remove the Con-Tact paper, lifting the edges with a sharp knife. Clean off any remaining adhesive with glass cleaner and paper towels. Mount the mirror in a frame (see the instructions on pages 30–31).

1.   2.   3.

faux leather frame

MATERIALS AND TOOLS

- flat-faced wood picture frame (to build your own, see instructions on pages 30–31)
- Anaglypta wallcovering or border, or any embossed paper
- scissors
- wallpaper paste or strong white glue
- bronze and black latex paint, satin
- 2" paintbrush
- soft, lint-free rags
- semigloss acrylic varnish
- foam brush

On a trip to Spain I discovered many of the stunning ways that leather can be used on furnishings. In that country, the leather is often embossed with an intricate pattern and then buffed to a deep sheen. I copied this look at a fraction of the cost by gluing pieces of Anaglypta, an embossed wallcovering, to a large flat frame and then highlighting the pattern with bronze and black paint. The effect is as dramatic as real leather.

INSTRUCTIONS

STEP 1. Cut the Anaglypta into strips slightly longer and wider than each piece of the frame. Spread wallpaper paste on the back of each strip and press into place. Make diagonal cuts at the corners and fold the paper over the sides and onto the back of each frame. Hold for 1 to 3 minutes until thoroughly adhered.

STEP 2. Brush on 1 coat of bronze paint, making sure to get into all the creases. Let dry overnight.

STEP 3. Brush on 1 solid coat of black paint, once again being sure to get into all the creases. While the black paint is still wet, rub the surface with a rag, removing the black from the top to expose the bronze layer, but leaving black behind in the creases. Work in small areas so that the black doesn't dry before you have time to rub it off. This technique accentuates the intricate pattern of the embossed paper.

STEP 4. Apply 1 coat of varnish for sheen.

lovers' frame

MATERIALS AND TOOLS
- ½" MDF
- black marker
- jigsaw
- mask
- water-based primer
- paintbrush or foam brush
- pencil

BASE COAT
- cream latex paint, matte or satin
- foam brush

FINISH
- fine-line and thick indelible gold pens
- eraser
- raw sienna artist's acrylic paint
- water
- soft, lint-free rag
- acrylic varnish
- foam brush
- 8 mirror clips

When my brother got married, I made him and his new bride this romantic framed mirror. Using a template, I cut a large piece of MDF with a jigsaw into a wiggly, uneven pattern. I cut the center out and had a piece of beveled mirror cut to size, which was held in place with mirror clips. With an indelible gold marker, I wrote an edited history of their short life together around the frame, and then I rubbed on raw sienna artist's acrylic to antique the frame. Always do a small test with markers to make sure they will not run when you apply the varnish.

My gift was received with huge enthusiasm. Since then I've used the idea for wedding anniversaries, new baby arrivals, and a housewarming. Instead of a mirror you can also frame a special photograph or picture.

INSTRUCTIONS

STEP 1. Draw out a pattern for the frame on the MDF with a black marker. Cut out the frame with a jigsaw; be sure to wear a mask.

STEP 2. Apply 1 coat of primer to both sides of the frame and let dry for 2 to 3 hours.

STEP 3. Apply 2 coats of cream base coat and let dry for 4 hours.

STEP 4. Write the words you have chosen around the frame in pencil.

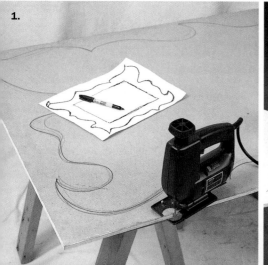

1.

4.

5.

Then trace around the penciled words with the thick and thin gold pens. Let dry. Remove any visible pencil marks with an eraser.

STEP 5. Put a dab of raw sienna artist's acrylic in a dish and dilute it with a little water; it should be very thin. Fold a soft rag and dip it into the diluted color. Rub the color very lightly over the entire frame, moving in one direction. The finish on the frame should look slightly streaky.

STEP 6. When the finish is dry, add 2 coats of varnish for protection.

STEP 7. Turn the frame over and attach the mirror from the back using mirror clips.

1.

3.

lace picture frame

MATERIALS AND TOOLS

- square paper doilies
- photograph
- scissors
- sharp X-acto knife
- cutting mat
- white craft glue
- 2 pieces of glass the same size
- 1″ colored masking tape, we used standard cream

This easy frame is nothing more than a paper doily and a photograph sandwiched between two pieces of glass. The delicacy of lace and the pureness of white paper give these picture frames an essence of bygone days. Doilies are available from supermarkets in a variety of sizes, and they can also be cut to fit your picture as I have done here. The glass frame is held together with a neat masking-tape border and is designed to sit on a plate stand.

INSTRUCTIONS

STEP 1. To make a custom-sized doily: Cut a doily in half and overlap the two halves until the shape is the right size for your photograph. Cut out the excess in the middle with the X-acto knife, trimming neatly around the doily pattern. Leave a small overlap.

STEP 2. Glue the two halves together along the overlap. Glue the photo to the center of the doily.

STEP 3. Clean the glass well. Insert the framed photo between the two pieces of glass.

STEP 4. Cut 4 strips of masking tape and wrap 1 piece along each edge to create an even border around the sides of the frame. This will hold the glass, the doily, and the picture together.

bathroom cabinet frame

Instead of removing an unattractive medicine cabinet mirror from the bathroom wall, I dressed it up by stenciling a frame around it with paint and ornamental gesso. The gesso creates a raised pattern that's highlighted by lightly brushing over the surface with gold paint. If you're stenciling with either plaster or gesso, keep the design simple. Otherwise the stencil is difficult to remove from the wet plaster. Ornamental gesso, unlike artist's gesso or plaster, has an elasticity agent in it which allows it to "move" with changes in humidity. Unless plaster is skim-coated onto a surface, it will crack.

MATERIALS AND TOOLS

- stencil design
- Mylar
- fine indelible black marker
- sharp X-acto knife
- cutting mat
- pencil
- spray adhesive
- ornamental gesso
- small plaster trowel or spatula
- rag

PAINTED FINISH

- low-tack painter's tape
- red artist's acrylic paint
- water-based glazing liquid
- mixing container
- 1" paintbrush
- soft, lint-free rag
- gold metallic artist's acrylic paint
- artist's brush

RECIPE

- 2 parts artist's acrylic paint
- 1 part water-based glazing liquid

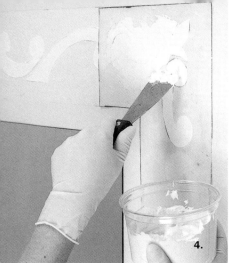

INSTRUCTIONS

STEP 1. Choose a design and make a stencil of it. Cut the stencil out using a sharp X-acto knife and a cutting mat. It's a good idea to cut two as the stencil must be washed and dried each time it is used. Tape off an 8″ border on the wall around the mirror.

STEP 2. Plan where your stencil design will go around the mirror and mark the positions with a pencil.

STEP 3. Spray the back of the stencil with adhesive and press it into position flat against the wall.

STEP 4. Using a spatula, smear the gesso over the stencil about ¼″ thick. Carefully remove the stencil, leaving behind an embossed pattern.

STEP 5. Wash the back of the stencil each time you use it and dry off with a rag. Continue stenciling with the gesso around the mirror until your design is completed. Let the gesso dry for 24 hours.

STEP 6. Mix the colored glaze. Using a 1″ paintbrush, apply the glaze to the frame area covering everything, including all the embossed stencil design.

STEP 7. With a soft rag, dab over the raised design to diminish any brushstrokes. Let the glaze dry. A second coat can be added once dry to add more depth to the color.

STEP 8. To highlight the design, reposition the stencil and brush on a little gold metallic paint with an artist's brush.

mosaic mirror frame

Mosaic is an ancient art form in which broken pieces of ceramics are applied to any flat surface in a pattern and secured into place with tile grout. On this unusually shaped frame I wanted to create a reflective mosaic. Irregular pieces of mirrored glass were the answer. To fill the spaces between the glass, I used mastic putty, which I painted silver. This gives the interesting effect of old leaded windows with a contemporary shape.

MATERIALS AND TOOLS

- flat-faced wood frame
- piece of mirror approximately the size of the frame
- safety glasses
- work gloves
- pillowcase
- hammer
- tile adhesive
- mastic putty
- spatula
- gray and silver artist's acrylic paint
- artist's brush

INSTRUCTIONS

Note: Wear protective glasses when breaking the mirror. Mirror edges are sharp, so work gloves are recommended. Use a flat-faced frame following the instructions on pages 30–31.

STEP 1. Place the mirror inside a pillowcase. Carefully hit it with a hammer to produce irregular pieces 1″–2″ in size.

STEP 2. Apply tile adhesive to the frame, one section at a time, and then lay down mirror pieces, leaving a small space around each for putty. Let dry overnight.

STEP 3. Follow the directions on the package of mastic putty, kneading it well before opening the package. Roll the putty into long lines to make it easier to maneuver around the mirror edges. Fill in the spaces snugly with putty.

STEP 4. Once all the spaces have been filled, paint can be applied even while the putty is still wet. Mix a little gray and silver paint together and paint the putty to replicate the leading in a glass window. It may take as long as a week or two to dry thoroughly. Be sure to keep it in a dry place, as humidity impedes drying.

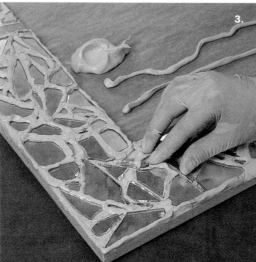
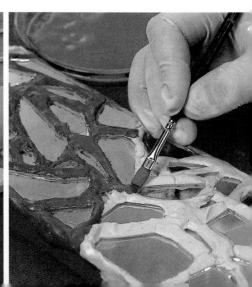

2.

3.

4.

poster headboard

MATERIALS AND TOOLS

- poster
- ½" MDF, the width of the bed, plus extra for cutting 2 legs
- wallpaper paste
- 2 lengths of 1" × 2" wood, the length of the legs plus height of the poster
- screws
- screwdriver
- primer
- bolts, if attaching the poster frame to the bed
- stock molding for frame
- miter box
- aqua and white latex paint, satin
- paintbrush
- hot-glue gun and glue sticks
- finishing nails
- hammer

Instead of hanging a poster in the traditional way, I created a headboard using an image from a favorite artist. This Georgia O'Keeffe poster was blown up to the width of a queen-size bed, framed and laminated, so it is easy to clean. The effect is dramatic and quite beautiful.

INSTRUCTIONS

STEP 1. Cut a piece of MDF the exact size of the poster. (It should be the width of your bed.) Using wallpaper paste, glue the poster to the MDF. Posters can be blown up to any size.

STEP 2. Cut from MDF 2 legs that are 4" wide and long enough to reach just beneath the top edge of the mattress (ours are 18"). Cut two 2" wood strips the length of the poster height plus the length of a leg. Screw the wood strips to the back of the poster and legs to secure the two pieces together. Paint the back of the MDF with primer to seal it.

STEP 3. Measure and cut 4 lengths of stock molding the length and width of the picture. Miter the corners (see page 31). Prime the molding and apply 1 aqua base coat. When dry, add a little white paint pulled across the surface to distress the color.

STEP 4. Use a hot-glue gun and finishing nails to attach the picture frame around the edges of the poster. *Note:* You can also hang the headboard frame above the bed just like a picture (you will not need the legs).

lighting

Lighting is not only a necessity, it's a powerful decorating tool. Creative lighting can transform a room, highlight a favorite object, camouflage a less impressive area, or make a room look grander, cozier, or more romantic. The variety of lighting available is endless, from high-tech halogens to traditional lamps and an enormous choice in candles.

The quandaries start when you try to find a lamp or shade that will complement your decor. Typically, lampshades are very plain and boring. There are businesses that will design a shade to coordinate with your fabric or room style, but this can be a costly undertaking.

Designing your own lampshade takes little time, and because shades are small and the materials required are easy to find, it's one of the simplest projects. Basic shades are available at lighting and craft stores or you can cut out a shade from lightweight poster board or heavy paper. Most mediums can be used for decoration: paint, paper, and fabric. Then accessorize with beads and fringe. Here's the place to splurge on fabulous material and trim, as you need so little.

Candleholders can be customized as well with individual shades created for a special occasion. And I've also included a simple design for a pioneer-style candle sconce cut from metal. Remember to ensure that any candleholders are well secured, and never leave lit candles unattended.

A lamp can be made from just about anything: a memorable bottle of champagne, decorative tins, or an antique silver coffeepot. You can have an object wired professionally or buy a wiring kit at the hardware or lighting store and do it yourself.

sexy spanish shades

Only dramatic shades would be suitable for this wrought-iron chandelier that hangs in a Spanish-themed dining room. To match the rich palette of the walls, I used a sexy fabric called burnt-out velvet. Areas of the black velvet where the design has been burnt out are transparent, so the red cardboard shade can be seen beneath it. I completed the look with a lush trim.

INSTRUCTIONS

STEP 1. Use the template to draw the shape of the shade on cardboard (see the transferring instructions on page 185). Cut out the shade with a sharp knife or scissors. This size template will fit the standard bulb clip.

STEP 2. Paint one side of the cardboard shade red. Let dry.

STEP 3. Cut out a piece of velvet using the same template, adding a ½″ allowance to the top for overlap. Glue the fabric to the shade by dotting craft

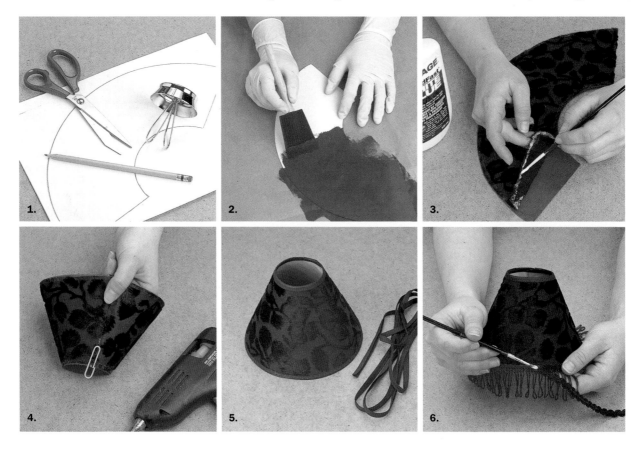

MATERIALS AND TOOLS

- a bulb clip for an electric chandelier, available at lighting and hardware stores
- template for shade (page 189)
- tracing paper
- pencil
- carbon paper
- cardboard or thick paper
- sharp X-acto knife or scissors
- red latex paint, satin or semigloss
- small brush
- ½ yard black burnt-out velvet
- white craft glue
- paper clips
- 1½' black bias tape
- 1' red fringe
- scissors
- hot-glue gun and glue stick

glue in places it won't be visible (not on sheer areas). Glue down the overlap to the inside top of the shade.

STEP 4. Paper-clip the lampshade form and leave overnight so that it takes shape. This makes it easier to glue together. Remove the clips and run a bead of hot glue down the overlap seam. Reclip until dry and solidly attached. The small circle should sit perfectly over the bulb clip.

STEP 5. Cut black bias tape to fit the top and bottom borders. Attach the tape using the hot-glue gun, beginning and ending at the lampshade seam.

STEP 6. Cut and hot-glue red fringe to the bottom of the shade starting at the seam. Follow with a piece of bias tape.

amaretto-cookie shade

1.

2.

4.

MATERIALS AND TOOLS

- white paper lampshade
- Amaretto cookie wrappers or tissue paper
- iron
- cotton tea towel
- scissors
- spray adhesive
- white craft glue
- satin water-based varnish
- foam brush
- hot-glue gun and glue sticks
- chainette fringe and white cord the circumference of the shade
- raw egg (optional)

I came across a box of delicious after-dinner cookies in an Italian delicatessen. Not only were the cookies divine, but so were the wrappings —delicate printed tissue paper in a variety of pastel shades. I used the wrappers to cover a plain paper lampshade, added some fringe from a local craft store, and then fashioned an unusual finial: an empty eggshell protected with four coats of varnish. The shade is gorgeous, and as a perk you get to eat the whole box of cookies to be able to use the papers!

INSTRUCTIONS

STEP 1. Iron the wrappers until they are wrinkle free. Tissue will burn easily, so press them under a tea towel; do not apply the hot iron directly to the tissue.

STEP 2. Lightly spray the back of a wrapper with adhesive and press it onto the lampshade. Repeat until the whole shade is covered. You may have to cut wrappers to fit spaces rather than overlapping them, as the paper is so thin that you would see one color through the other, but that isn't necessary. Secure any loose corners with craft glue; let dry completely.

STEP 3. Apply 4 coats of water-based varnish.

STEP 4. Using the hot-glue gun, apply a bead of glue around the bottom edge of the lampshade and press on the chainette border. Start and end at the lampshade's seam.

STEP 5. Apply white cord to the top of the shade in the same manner.

STEP 6. If you want to use an eggshell for a finial, prick the raw egg at either end with a needle and blow out the white and yolk. Make the hole on one end large enough to fit over the screw that will hold the finial. Let the shell dry out and apply 4 coats of varnish to strengthen it.

silhouette shade

Silhouettes were popular with the Victorians as framed portraits, but silhouetting is an art form that can be adapted in numerous ways, especially for decorating. Inspired by the style of the Adirondacks, I transformed an inexpensive paper lampshade with this wilderness silhouette. When the light is off, the effect is simply a matte ochre finish. When the light is switched on, the silhouette scene magically appears.

INSTRUCTIONS

STEP 1. As each shade varies in size and shape, you will have to make your own template to fit. Lay the black construction paper on a flat surface,

MATERIALS AND TOOLS

- white paper lampshade
- 1 large sheet black construction paper
- colored wax pencil
- tracing paper
- photocopies of chosen design or use ours (template on page 189)
- spray adhesive
- scissors and sharp X-acto knife
- craft glue
- yellow ocher latex paint, satin
- soft, lint-free rag

hold the lampshade on its side on top of the paper, and trace the lower edge with a colored pencil as you roll the shade. Start at the shade's seam and when you have returned to the seam, add another ¼″ for overlap. Follow the same procedure to trace the top edge of the shade. Cut out the template.

STEP 2. Make photocopies of images taken from magazines, reference books, or snapshots, or use the design provided on page 189.

STEP 3. Cut out a piece of tracing paper the same shape as your black template. Lay the tracing paper over the images you have chosen, tracing a design scene around the tracing paper template.

STEP 4. Use spray adhesive to adhere the tracing paper design to the black construction paper template. Cut out around the design with scissors and an X-acto knife for fine cut work. Remove the tracing paper from the black template.

STEP 5. Spray the adhesive to the inside of the shade. Affix the scene to the inside carefully, starting at the seam. Pull it tight and smooth down the cutouts as you move around the shade. Use craft glue to secure the edges.

STEP 6. With a rag, rub yellow ocher paint onto the outside of the shade to color and softly texture the surface.

bamboo lighting

The decorative style and materials of the Far East are increasingly popular in the West. Bamboo is renowned for its look and its strength, and it was the ideal base for my oriental-themed lamp. Bamboo is now readily available in different sized widths and lengths; here I used a large piece that was 4 inches in diameter. Bamboo is hard to cut, so you will need a small saw. I attached the bamboo to a wooden plinth painted the same color. Once the base was wired, it required an appropriate shade to complement the eastern theme. Chinese newspaper was a perfect choice, but it is preferable to use photocopies of the paper as newsprint can bleed when varnished. Cut the paper into work-able pieces and glue it to the surface of the shade. Lastly I rubbed a little green paint over the paper before applying three coats of varnish.

MATERIALS AND TOOLS

- small 2″ pine board
- handsaw or table saw
- router (optional)
- medium- and fine-grade sandpaper
- four 2½″ screws (for pedestal base)
- drill
- self-adhesive felt (protective material for table and chair feet)
- acrylic primer
- foam brush
- bamboo-color brown latex paint
- sea sponge or soft, lint-free rag
- lamp wiring kit
- carpenter's glue
- 2′ length of bamboo 4″–5″ in diameter
- Styrofoam

INSTRUCTIONS

STEP 1. To make the lamp pedestal, cut 2 pine squares, one smaller than the other. These edges were shaped and finished with a router, but you can simply sand the edges smooth. Join the two pieces together by inserting 2 screws through the bottom of the base. Countersink the screws. Attach self-adhesive felt to the bottom of the base.

STEP 2. Cut a knob of wood approximately 2″ high and slightly narrower than the bamboo's inner diameter; screw it to the top of the pedestal.

STEP 3. Drill holes for wiring: one from the center of the knob through the base and one from the side of the base to meet the central hole.

STEP 4. Prime the base and apply the bamboo-colored paint. Use a rag or a sea sponge to give the paint a little texture. Let dry.

STEP 5. Feed the lamp wire through the base and up the center.

STEP 6. Apply carpenter's glue to the outside of the knob and around its base as well as to the edge and inner circumference of the bamboo. With the wire running up through the bamboo, lower the bamboo over the knob onto the base and twist it until it is snug and secure.

STEP 7. Cut a Styrofoam circle that will fit snugly into the top of the bamboo and make a hole in the center of the circle. Feed the wire through the circle and then press it into the top of the bamboo.

STEP 8. Finish wiring the lamp following the kit's instructions.

4.

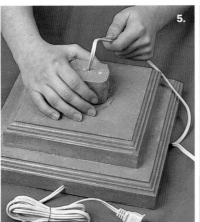

5.

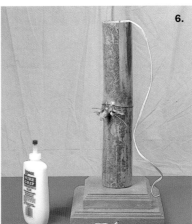

6.

7.

pioneer tin candleholders

MATERIALS AND TOOLS

- graph paper
- candles
- pencil and ruler
- tin snippers
- masking tape
- sheet of tin
- work gloves
- sandpaper for metal
- wood board
- 3″ nail for punching holes
- hammer
- 2″ brackets, 2 per sconce
- two 1″ metal screws
- metal cupcake molds
- metallic spray paint, copper
- black spray paint
- 3″ nails for attaching the sconce to the wall

Punched tin has been used for generations by folk artists for decorative objects. This simple technique requires little more than a nail and hammer and sheet of tin. I found the shiny silver of the tin too modern for these candleholders, so I applied an antiqued copper patina as a finishing touch.

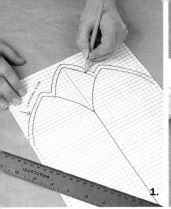
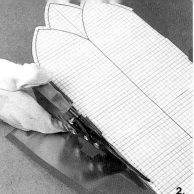
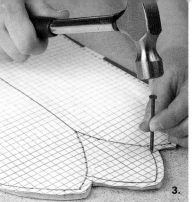
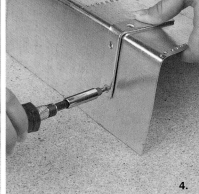

1.

2.

3.

4.

5.

6.

INSTRUCTIONS

Note: You can place one or two candles on this sconce; just adjust your design and the number of brackets accordingly.

STEP 1. Draw out the pattern you want on a piece of graph paper. Determine the length of the sconce by measuring the height of the candles you will be using plus the depth of the shelf that is turned up to hold the candles. Add 2″ to the length of the candle measurement and 3″ for the shelf. We used an 8″ candle, so the length of the sconce is $8 + 2 + 3 = 13″$.

STEP 2. Cut out the pattern and place pencil dots ¼″ apart and ¼″ inset around the pattern edges and along the pattern design lines. Tape the pattern to a sheet of tin and cut the tin to size using tin snippers. Wear heavy-duty protective gloves, as the metal edges are sharp. Sand the edges of the tin smooth.

STEP 3. With the paper pattern still attached, place the tin on a wood board. Use a 3″ nail and a hammer to puncture the tin along the pencil dots. Make sure the nail goes cleanly through each dot. Stop the pattern 3″ from the bottom.

STEP 4. To make the shelf, mark 3″ up from the bottom of the sconce on both sides and then bend the tin over a straight-edged piece of wood. Secure it in place with 2 small brackets. Each bracket is held in place with 1 metal screw that is screwed through the shelf along the midline. This screw will stick up on the other side.

STEP 5. With hammer and nail, make a hole at the bottom of a metal cupcake mold and drop the mold over the screw. This screw will also hold the candle in place. Predrilled candles are available, or it's possible to simply twist the solid candle base onto the screw.

STEP 6. Apply a light, uneven coat of both copper spray paint and black spray paint to the sconce to give it an aged smoky patina.

STEP 7. Attach the sconce to the wall with the same size nails you used to punch the tin. Hammer through holes already punctured in the pattern.

141

south seas sconce

Plaster light sconces are designed as wall fixtures that can either be painted to blend in with your wall or decorated with any finish to build on a particular style. When I was painting a bathroom that had a beautiful Balinese-style mirror, I enhanced the plain plaster sconces to match the South Seas theme. Lines of glue from a glue gun and coffee beans added a relief effect, and the whole thing was painted with a rusty finish.

INSTRUCTIONS

For the best results, prepare your surface following the guidelines in the preparation section, page 41.

STEP 1. Apply 2 coats of terra-cotta base coat to the sconce and let dry for 4 hours.

STEP 2. Mix the burnt umber colored glaze and sponge it over the sconce. Hold the sconce upright and drizzle a little water over the top. As the water runs down, it will create a streaky effect in the patina. Let dry.

STEP 3. Using the hot-glue gun, draw a relief pattern in glue over the surface of the sconce. Let the glue pattern dry.

STEP 4. Add to the design by gluing individual coffee beans onto the surface of the sconce. Let dry.

MATERIALS AND TOOLS
- plaster sconce
- terra-cotta latex paint, satin
- paintbrush
- burnt umber artist's acrylic paint
- water-based glazing liquid
- mixing container
- small paintbrush or foam brush, kitchen sponge or sea sponge
- hot-glue gun and glue sticks
- coffee beans
- black spray paint
- matte spray varnish

RECIPE
- a squirt of artist's acrylic paint
- 1 cup water-based glazing liquid

3.

4.

5.

STEP 5. Paint over the top, alternating between sponging on a terra-cotta glaze and spraying black paint, building up the rust effect and covering the beans and glue.

STEP 6. Apply 2 coats of matte spray varnish.

fabrics and floorcoverings

One of the most expensive areas of decorating concerns the use of fabrics. Whether for window coverings, upholstery, or cushions, beautiful fabrics can, and often do, cost a fortune. While you may be renting your home, and unwilling to spend a lot on new curtains or blinds, chances are you will need something to cover the windows for practical purposes. Luckily, there are many affordable plain fabrics that can be painted, stenciled, stamped, dyed, and even metallic-leafed to give your room a stylish look. And it's not at all difficult to put the projects in this section together, even if you can't sew.

Clever new drapery hardware and sewing aides, together with creative swagging and tucking techniques, have revolutionized the way we dress windows and upholster chairs. You no longer require a sewing machine to fashion beautiful soft furnishings for your home.

Just like fabrics, floor coverings can also be expensive, but there are some inspiring alternatives. Decorative floorcloths, for example, are art on the floor. They can be walked on, cleaned easily, and taken with you when you move. Inexpensive sisal is extremely durable and usually available in natural colors. It's perfect to personalize with paint and a stencil in any pattern to fit your decor.

Ticking fabric still on the roll was attached by Velcro to the window trim as a quick window treatment.

daisy drapes

MATERIALS AND TOOLS

- 2 lengths of contrasting fabric
  (fabric to be heat-cut must be
  100% polyester)
- chosen design or daisy pattern
  (template on page 187)
- Mylar
- fine indelible black marker
- sharp X-acto knife
- cutting mat
- straight pins
- tapestry hoop
- stencil burning tool, available
  at craft stores
- sheet of glass
- masking tape
- pencil
- sewing machine and thread

These café au lait curtains are as light and breezy as a summer's day, yet provide full privacy for French doors. I reversed the usual order and layered frothy sheer fabric over a solid coffee-toned lining. The idea was to have two fabrics, one as backdrop that would show through a lighter sheer where a design has been cut out. To cut the pattern, I used a stencil burner, which cuts very quickly and neatly and seals the edges so that the fabric won't fray. But you must use a polyester fabric for the heat to melt and seal the edges around the design.

INSTRUCTIONS

For yardage requirements and construction information, see tips for making simple curtains, page 35.

STEP 1. For the sheer, top layer of fabric: Draw a design or photocopy the daisy template to the desired size (see page 187). You could draw your design freehand directly onto the fabric, but the stencil will ensure the repeats are alike.

STEP 2. Lay out the fabric and decide where you are going to place the cutout designs and mark the positions on the fabric with pins.

STEP 3. Use a tapestry hoop to hold the fabric taut. Work over a piece of glass, as the stencil burner is very hot and will damage wood, plastic, and rubber. Place the hoop face down so the fabric is flush with the glass. Tape the stencil to the fabric and draw the pattern with a pencil. Remove the stencil.

3.

4.

5.

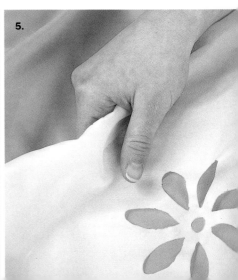

STEP 4. Using the burning tool, carefully cut out the design. Move to the next designated position and repeat.

STEP 5. Slide the second layer of fabric, in a contrasting color, underneath the cutout to see the effect.

STEP 6. To make up the curtains, with right sides together, sew the sheer to the contrasting liner at the sides and top (see instructions for making a cushion, page 36). Turn and press seams flat. Sew a rod pocket at the top and hem the bottom (see page 35), as required.

MATERIALS AND TOOLS

- white cotton muslin
- ruler or tape measure
- straight pins
- paper clips
- large metal pot
- water to fill pot
- gray fabric dye
- salt
- stove
- tongs
- iron
- sewing machine and thread or hemming tape

tie-dye curtains

The owners of this city loft did not want to block the gorgeous natural light that streams through the huge windows, but they did want some privacy. Sheer fabric was the answer, but to make it more interesting I

hand-dyed white muslin with a delicate pattern. The fabric was cut into long lengths and then folded into accordion pleats held in place with a line of paper clips. Each section was soaked in a bath of fabric dye; when the fabric was removed, the folds and clip marks remained white while the rest of the fabric took on the smoky gray color. The panels were then clipped onto rings and suspended from a fine curtain wire. The oversized swags and the excess of fabric pooling on the floor are modern, luxurious touches.

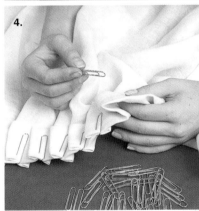

INSTRUCTIONS

For yardage requirements and construction information, see tips for making simple curtains, page 35. *Note:* Many different patterns can be achieved with tie-dye, which is a negative-positive technique. Try tying golf balls or marbles to the fabric to create circles. This is done by wrapping a section of the fabric around the object and securing it with an elastic band.

STEP 1. Cut muslin curtain panels to chosen length.

STEP 2. Lay the fabric out on a long table or the floor. Make a 1½″ fold along one of the long edges. Hold the fold in place with straight pins.

STEP 3. Return to the same edge and fold the length over again, removing the pins and repinning the double fold.

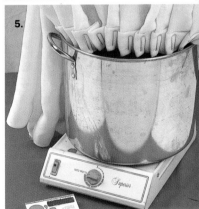

STEP 4. Go to the top of the fabric, this time working across the width of the panel. Make a 1″-deep pleat in the already folded fabric, removing the straight pins and securing the pleat with a paper clip. Make another inch-wide pleat right up against the first one and secure it with a paper clip. Continue to the bottom of the fabric. I did this technique every 12″, which creates large strips of solid and broken color.

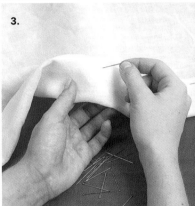

STEP 5. Fill up a large metal pot with water and add the fabric dye, following the directions on the package. Make sure to add salt, which acts as a fixative. Immerse the paper-clipped panels, boil on the stove according to instructions on the dye package, remove with tongs, and hang to dry.

STEP 6. Once the fabric is dry, remove the paper clips.

STEP 7. Lightly press with an iron on low heat to remove the fold lines. Turn under the raw edges and hem them using a machine or hemming tape.

damask curtains

Over the last five years a variety of patterned rollers have come onto the market. Designed mainly for applying patterns directly onto walls, they can also be used for decorating furnishings and fabric. They're huge fun to use and the image is produced so quickly, you can have your curtains hung almost immediately. These patterned rollers are actually two rollers attached together; one is a standard foam roller that is loaded with paint from a paint tray. The second, a patterned rubber roller, rolls over the surface of the foam roller and the paint feeds evenly onto the rubber surface. This keeps the pattern from fading out as the roller is used. Here, I chose a damask design to border plain cotton curtains. For a permanent washable finish you can use fabric paint; otherwise, latex paint is good for short-term makeovers.

INSTRUCTIONS

For yardage requirements and construction information, see tips for making simple curtains, page 35.

STEP 1. Lay fabric lengthwise on a table or floor. Tape the edge of the fabric to your surface to be sure it is taut and won't slip.

STEP 2. Pour some paint into the paint tray and tip the tray so that the paint covers the top of the tray as well. Roll the sponge roller, not the rubber patterned roller, through the paint. You will see that the sponge roller sits slightly lower than the rubber roller.

STEP 3. Roll a couple of times on scrap paper to load the patterned roller with paint. You get only one chance to apply the border to the fabric, so practice until you feel confident.

MATERIALS AND TOOLS

- cotton or linen fabric
- masking tape
- taupe latex or fabric paint
- paint tray
- patterned roller
- scrap paper
- iron

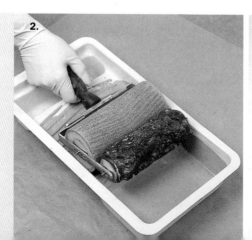

STEP 4. Roll onto the fabric in one continuous stroke, pressing down firmly. Be sure that only the patterned roller touches the fabric. Let dry.

STEP 5. If you have used fabric paint, heat-set the dry pattern with an iron following the manufacturer's instructions.

tranquil sheers

MATERIALS AND TOOLS

- sheer fabric
- low-tack painter's tape
- ruler
- 1″ paintbrush
- antique gold and silver fabric paint
- rubber stamp
- spare fabric
- iron

Sheers have grown immensely popular and you can now buy these delicate fabrics not only in numerous colors but also with a variety of patterns woven into the material. These patterned sheers can be costly, but you can reproduce the look by decorating your own plain fabric. Stamps are an ideal way to produce a uniform design. Use fabric paint and practice first on a spare piece to get the feel of working with the paint and fabric. Here I first hung venetian blinds to control the light. The stamped sheers were attached by sewing satin loops in intervals along the top of each panel and hanging each one over a decorative drawer pull screwed to the wall. The flowing sheers soften the hard lines of the venetian blinds behind.

INSTRUCTIONS

For yardage requirements and construction information, see tips for making simple curtains, page 35.

STEP 1. Lay the fabric out on a flat surface and measure and mark where the pattern will be stamped with a ruler and low-tack tape.

STEP 2. With a small brush apply a little of each paint evenly onto the stamp. Practice on an extra piece of fabric first to get the right amount of paint on the stamp.

STEP 3. Remove the tape, one piece at a time, and press the stamp straight down firmly onto the fabric. Lift the stamp off, pulling the stamp straight up so the paint won't smudge. Reapply paint to the stamp and repeat the process to complete the desired pattern. Let dry.

STEP 4. Iron to heat-set the paint following the manufacturer's instructions.

1.   2.   3.   4.

exotic canopy

MATERIALS AND TOOLS

- sheer fabric, the width and twice the length of the bed
- cardboard
- scissors
- pencil and ruler
- low-tack painter's tape
- cutting mat and plastic wrap
- metallic size
- 1″ paintbrush
- silver leaf
- soft bristle brush

This rather sexy bed canopy was fashioned from a few yards of inexpensive red sheer fabric and silver leaf. The leaf is glued in random squares onto both sides of the fabric so that the silver can be seen from inside and outside the bed; this technique also hides the glue behind each square. The shimmering canopy is draped over metal rods that are hung from cords attached to the ceiling.

INSTRUCTIONS

Sew the fabric together to make a canopy the correct width and length for your bed.

STEP 1. Cut a cardboard square about ⅛″ smaller than a square of the silver leaf. Use this as a template to measure the squares on the fabric. Mark around the square with a pencil and ruler and tape it off with low-tack tape following a random pattern.

STEP 2. Work on a flat surface. Because the glue will seep through the sheer fabric, cover a cutting mat with plastic wrap and slip it under the fabric. Brush a thin layer of the size onto the fabric inside the masked squares. Repeat for all the squares. Leave it for approximately ½ hour until the size is almost dry, but still tacky to the touch.

STEP 3. Carefully lay a sheet of silver leaf onto the tacky square. Let dry about ½ hour, then gently brush back and forth across the leaf with a soft brush. Remove the tape.

STEP 4. Turn the fabric over. Following the instructions for the first side, tape off, apply size, and adhere the silver leaf to the backs of the squares you have finished. The sheer fabric is thin, so you must apply the leaf to both sides.

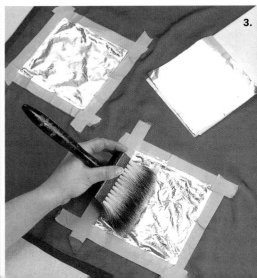

screen print slipcovers

MATERIALS AND TOOLS
- canvas for slipcover
- small prestretched silk screen
- wax paper
- scissors
- cardboard or cutting mat
- sharp X-acto knife
- several drawings or photocopies of chosen image
- masking tape
- water-based textile ink
- squeegee no less than 2″ wider than your image
- water and household cleaner
- iron

Dining room chairs have a habit of going out of date every ten years, but to replace a whole set at once is not always possible. The best solution is slipcovers, and just about any shape chair can be covered. Follow the generic instructions for making a slipcover on pages 38–39, and adapt them to your own chairs. Then you can add the decoration. Here I screen-printed a leaf design on the back of each cover. It takes practice to screen-print large or multicolored designs, but single images such as flowers, urns, or geometric shapes can easily be printed using small screens, which are available in art supply stores.

INSTRUCTIONS

For yardage requirements and sewing instructions, see pages 38–39.

Practice screen printing on a spare piece of the material you are using for this project. The number of times you are required to draw the ink down varies with the fabric type and the desired intensity of color.

STEP 1. Place the image you wish to duplicate on a cutting mat. Over this, place a piece of wax paper. Using an X-acto knife, cut around the edge of the image to

**MATERIALS
AND TOOLS**

- raw silk, enough to cover the seat plus a 2″ allowance
- stencil of chosen design
- masking tape
- black fabric paint
- stencil brush
- iron
- straight pins
- staple gun
- protective fabric spray

One of the best ways to give old dining room chairs a new look is to reupholster the seats. These rattan-backed Provençal-style chairs were in good condition, but the seats had a floral pattern that did not suit the room's oriental decor. Rather than replace the chairs, I chose an elegant raw silk fabric and stenciled the Chinese symbol for good health onto the center of each seat cushion (see page 188 for a template or choose your own design). Be sure to pick fabric that is suitable for upholstering, and once you have decorated the piece, treat it with a protective spray.

INSTRUCTIONS

STEP 1. Remove seat from chair. Cut the fabric to fit the seat plus 2″ on each side for overlap.

STEP 2. Lay the fabric on a flat surface. Center the stencil onto the fabric and tape in place. Fill in the image with black fabric paint and a stencil brush, using very little paint to avoid leakage. Blot excess from brush onto paper towel; use a circular motion to work paint into fibers. It is better to build up the color gradually.

STEP 3. When the image is dry, iron to heat-set the paint, following the manufacturer's instructions.

STEP 4. Smooth out the fabric onto the seat and center the image. Pin the fabric to the seat along the top edge. Flip the seat over and staple the fabric to the back, pulling the edges tight, across the bias (diagonally) first and then side to side.

STEP 5. Staple the four sides, and then smoothly fold and staple the corners.

STEP 6. Apply protective fabric spray.

2.

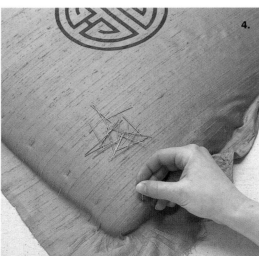

4.

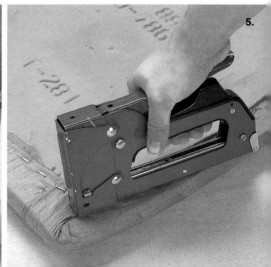

5.

pressed velvet cushions

The peacock is the national bird of India. So after I found some brightly colored tassels in an Indian store, I decided to stay with tradition and add a peacock feather to the velvet on these pillows. I used a stamping technique, not with paint, but with an iron. You must use a rubber stamp and the velvet must be made from silk, rayon, rayon acetate, or viscose. It's heat from the iron that makes the impression into the nap of the velvet, and it won't work on nylon, polyester, or washable velvets. The effect is marvelous and everyone who sees these cushions can't resist touching them.

INSTRUCTIONS

For this heating-printing technique, practice first on a scrap of velvet to get the right touch and heat time. The iron should be set at the wool or cotton setting. Avoid pressing down with the front of the iron as the steam holes will leave an impression. For instructions on how to make a cushion see page 36.

STEP 1. Cut out two pieces of velvet 1″ bigger than the size of cushion you want. Mark out your design on a piece of craft paper the size of the finished cushion using a pencil and ruler. Lay the paper on the back side of one piece of the velvet.

STEP 2. Lift up the craft paper and place pins where each design will go.

STEP 3. Heat your iron to the wool or cotton setting. Don't use any steam.

STEP 4. Place the stamp, rubber side up, on an ironing board. Lightly

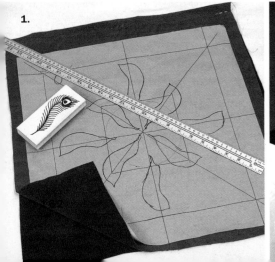

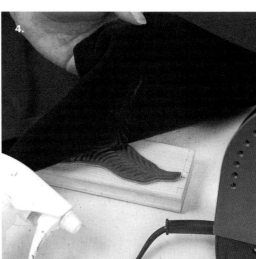

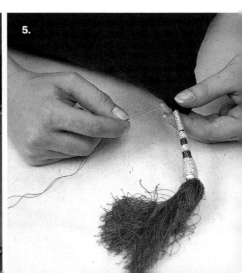

spray the back of the fabric with water. Remove a pin and lay the fabric right (velvet) side down against the rubber image. Press the iron to the back of the fabric and **DO NOT** move it. Count to 20 and lift up the iron carefully. The image has been impressed onto the velvet. Repeat until you have finished the pattern, and then do the same with the second piece of velvet.

STEP 5. Sew the pillow together, following the instructions on page 36. For a finishing touch I added tassels to the corners.

sackcloth cushions

MATERIALS AND TOOLS
- coffee-bean bags
- jute thread
- scissors
- needle and thread or sewing machine
- wool or tapestry needle
- masking tape
- fiberfill, sold by the bag at sewing and craft stores
- beads that resemble coffee beans (optional)

Forever on the lookout for unusual materials, I noticed a pile of empty coffee-bean bags thrown in the corner of my local coffee shop. The store owner looked at me a little strangely but on request gave me an armful of these sackcloth bags. They're quite beautiful and each one is printed differently. They need to be well washed, ironed, and then taken apart before beginning. Choose the part of the sack that is the most interesting. I added a jute cross-stitch around the edge and coffee-bean beads as a suitable trim.

INSTRUCTIONS

STEP 1. Unravel some thread from the sides of the jute coffee-bean bags and put them aside for step 4, the cross-stitch border.

STEP 2. Cut the bag to the size you want your pillow to be plus 1″ seam allowance all around. You should have two separate but equal-sized pieces of material. Choose pieces of sackcloth with the most interesting graphics.

STEP 3. Lay one piece of fabric on top of the other with right sides (the printed sides) together. Hand- or machine-sew the pillow together, leaving one side open. Clip the seams and turn it right side out.

STEP 4. Using the jute thread and a wool needle, sew a decorative cross-stitch along the three finished sides. To keep the stitches even, take a piece of masking tape the length of the pillow side and mark every inch along the tape. Apply the tape along the seams of the pillow as a stitch guideline. To

1.
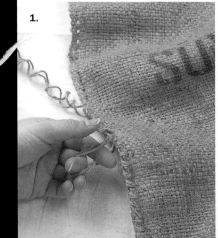

2.

4.

7.

make the cross-stitch, sew a diagonal stitch at each mark down one side, then come back stitching across the stitches to create Xs.

STEP 5. Stuff the pillowcase with fiberfill. Turn in the seam allowance on the open side and hand- or machine-stitch it closed.

STEP 6. Cross-stitch the fourth side.

STEP 7. At the corners, attach a bit of jute thread and string on a few beads for decoration.

2. **3.** **3.**

painted medieval sisal carpet

MATERIALS AND TOOLS

- sisal carpet
- low-tack painter's tape or chalk
- sheets of thick plastic or cardboard
- fine indelible black marker
- sharp X-acto knife
- cutting mat
- crown, shield, and fleur-de-lis patterns (templates on page 188)
- black, ultramarine blue, royal purple, red, and metallic gold latex paint, satin
- 3" paintbrush
- large stencil brush

Sisal is a matlike floor covering that is available in many different qualities. Rough-weave sisal is inexpensive and can be bought as runners or as rugs; the more expensive sisals are mixed with wool and are softer to the touch. They are available in a variety of natural shades. All sisal can be painted. In this room, a large open-weave sisal rug was given a medieval theme by stenciling bold homemade designs over the surface with latex paint. The pattern is very durable as the paint sinks deep into the weave. Practice first on a sample piece or the underside of the rug, as mistakes are difficult, if not impossible, to remove.

INSTRUCTIONS

STEP 1. Map out the pattern with tape or chalk. Make stencils of the patterns provided, following the instructions on page 185. When working on pile carpet or sisal the stencil needs to be thicker than traditional Mylar, so use thick plastic or cardboard.

STEP 2. Paint in the border using a 3" brush and latex paint. Use the paint liberally so that it goes into the weave.

STEP 3. Tape the stencils firmly into position and fill in the designs, swirling the stencil brush into the mat.

leafed canvas floorcloth

Before mass-produced carpets became popular in the nineteenth century, floorcloths were the poor man's alternative to expensive rugs. Most commonly used in rural areas, they were made from heavyweight canvas that was further stiffened with paint and varnish. Floorcloths are once again extremely popular. This is art on the floor that is perfect for a bathroom, hallway, or kitchen. Traditionally, they were either stenciled or hand-painted. I decided to take two of the newest materials available, colored metallic leaf and new dry adhesive sheets, to decorate this country floorcloth.

INSTRUCTIONS

To make a floorcloth, follow instructions on page 37.

    STEP 1. Apply 2 coats of lilac base coat over the primed floorcloth with a

MATERIALS AND TOOLS
- primed canvas floorcloth (see page 37 for instructions)
- mini-topiary stencils (templates on page 190) or purchased stencils
- lilac latex paint, satin
- roller and paint tray
- pencil, eraser, and ruler
- ⅛" low-tack painter's tape
- dry adhesive sheets (see Resources, page 191)
- blunt object for transferring adhesive (such as end of paintbrush)
- yellow green, olive green, crimson colored metal leaf (Japan leaf) (see Resources, page 191)
- small soft brush or 1" artist's brush
- water-based varnish
- 4" foam brush

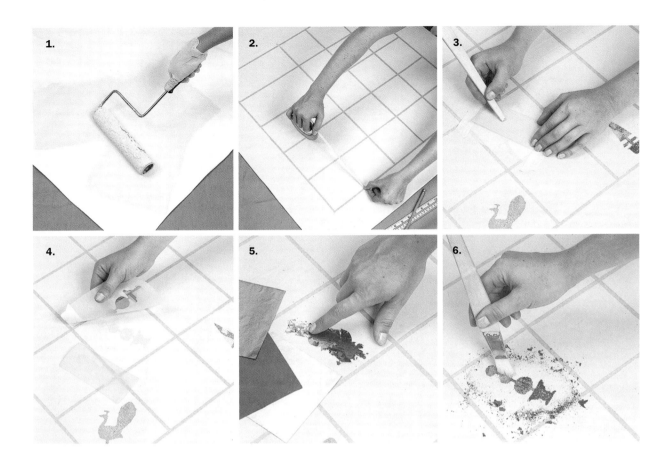

roller. Let dry overnight.

STEP 2. Work out a grid of 4–5″ squares, marking light dots with a pencil as a reference. Make the grid by placing the tape over the marks. This grid organizes the placement of the stencils so that you will have a balanced design.

STEP 3. Place a stencil in the center of a square and lay a piece of dry adhesive facedown over the stencil. Transfer the glue onto the painted canvas surface through the stencil hole by rubbing with a blunt object such as the end of a paintbrush.

STEP 4. Remove the adhesive strip and the stencil. The slightly sticky adhesive is now on the mat in the shape of your design.

STEP 5. Take a piece of the colored leaf about the size required to cover the motif, lay it in position over the adhesive, and gently press down. Here we did two colors at one time.

STEP 6. Using a soft brush, sweep the excess leaf away from the motif. Repeat for each motif and for the border.

STEP 7. Remove the tape and erase the pencil marks.

STEP 8. Apply 4 coats of varnish to protect the design.

garden furniture and accessories

We're spending more time and attention on gardening and relaxing outdoors, and our decorating skills have moved outside as well. Whether you have a country garden or a tiny city balcony, these places require some furniture, lighting, and accessories to enhance the flowers and greenery even more. Garden centers and lumber stores offer a treasure trove of materials and products that can be used outside the home.

Terra-cotta pots are sold in many shapes and sizes and can be decorated in as many ways as your imagination will allow. Now synthetic and galvanized metal pots and urns are available and ready for a paint finish. As long as the right primer is used, these inexpensive alternatives to the real thing can be just as gorgeous.

Wicker has long been a popular material for decks and gardens. Old pieces can be renewed or new pieces aged to suit your style. You can work on something as simple as a wind chime or as elaborate as a mosaic table. It's more fun than pulling weeds, and, as a bonus, the results can often be brought inside to brighten up your home during the winter.

Miniature picket fences were made by stapling together a row of pickets cut down to size and held in place with two bars along the back and one diagonally across the front. They were then whitewashed and painted with stenciled names.

picket flower box

MATERIALS AND TOOLS

- wooden flower box
- 10 or more loose picket fencing boards, depending on the size of the box
- handsaw or jigsaw
- latex primer
- white and black exterior latex paint, satin
- 2″ paintbrush
- artist's brush
- hot-glue gun and glue sticks
- finishing nails
- hammer

One of the distinguishing features of North American country gardens is the picket fence. Most hardware stores sell this fencing either as separate strips or already nailed together. Cut down to size, these miniature picket fences can be used in a variety of decorative ways around the garden. Here I dressed up a plain wooden flower box by nailing small pieces of pickets around the edge.

INSTRUCTIONS

STEP 1. Make or buy a plain wooden flower box. Using a handsaw, cut the picket fencing to measure 2″ higher than the flower box. Prime the flower box and fencing.

STEP 2. Apply one coat of white exterior paint. While it is still wet, paint black squiggles down the side of the box with an artist's brush.

STEP 3. Wipe over the designs gently with a dry brush to blend the black and white paint and create a weathered effect. Repeat this technique on all the fencing and let dry.

STEP 4. Attach each picket to the box with hot glue and secure into place with the finishing nails.

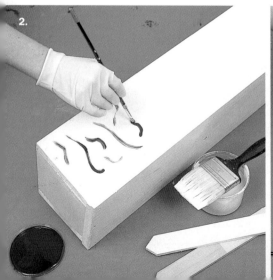

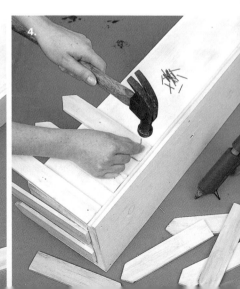

distressed wicker chairs

MATERIALS AND TOOLS
- spray white acrylic primer
- red and light green commercial or artist's acrylic paint, matte or satin
- 2" paintbrush
- soft, lint-free rags
- gloves

Resistant to wet weather and often more comfortable than wood, wicker furniture is ideal for the garden, balcony, or deck. Most of the wicker one finds at garage sales has been painted, and the paint has worn off over time. Today's new wicker pieces are usually sold raw, with no finish. I much prefer the look of faded old paint, as if these chairs have been sitting on a southern verandah in the summer heat. To give that aged look to this new chair, I first used a spray primer to seal the wicker, and then dry-brushed a couple of colors loosely over the surface.

INSTRUCTIONS

STEP 1. Spray the chair with a white acrylic primer and let dry. This is necessary whether the wicker is raw, already stained, varnished, or painted.

STEP 2. Apply red paint sparingly to the chair using a dry-brush technique. Dip the brush into the paint, then wipe most of the paint off on a rag. With almost dry bristles, rub the brush onto the wicker, applying the color in random patches.

STEP 3. Using a clean dry brush, apply the light green paint over the red, brushing on a slightly thicker coat. Rub back the chair with a soft rag to expose some of the red. Let dry.

mosaic garden table

sage so that the original is kept intact. Newspaper must be photocopied, as the newsprint will bleed when you apply glue and varnish.

Black-and-white photocopies can be hand-painted or stained for added effect. Color photocopies can also be used and are no longer very expensive to make.

Once the image is the right size, you will either want to transfer it onto the surface directly or use it to cut out a stencil.

TRACING AND TRANSFERRING AN IMAGE TO THE WORK SURFACE

It is not difficult to transfer an image directly to another surface.

STEP 1. Lay a piece of tracing paper over the image and trace the outline with a pencil.

STEP 2. Lay carbon paper, sometimes called transfer paper, carbon side down onto the surface where you want the image to be and then position the traced image face up on top of the carbon paper. Tape it in place. (It helps to position the traced image first so that you can see exactly where it's going, and then slide the carbon paper between the tracing paper and the surface.)

STEP 3. Draw over the traced image with a pencil and your design will be transferred onto the surface.

If the image you are tracing is a photocopy, you don't need tracing paper. Lay the photocopy directly over the carbon paper.

TO MAKE A STENCIL

It is always a good idea to make an extra stencil or two for backup. This is most important when stenciling with ornamental gesso, as the stencil must be washed and dried after each use. Small tears can be mended with tape.

If you are cutting out a stencil with a large space in the middle or letters such as "D," you will have to add a bridge so that the hole won't fall out. After you have stenciled the image onto your surface, remove the stencil, and tape off and fill in the bridge if it is large, or simply fill in small bridges by hand.

Some general cutting tips are to make as many long, continuous strokes as possible to avoid jagged edges, turn the Mylar rather than the knife, and hold the knife at a 45-degree angle to the surface.

TO CUT AND APPLY A STENCIL WITH A BRIDGE

STEP 1. Tape the photocopied image to your work surface. Place a sheet of Mylar over the image and tape it down securely. Trace the image onto the Mylar with a fine indelible marker.

The letter "D" requires a small bridge at the top and bottom.

STEP 2. Tape the Mylar to a cutting mat and cut out the stencil with a sharp X-acto knife.

STEP 3. Apply your stencil to your decorated surface with a stencil brush.

STEP 4. Remove the Mylar stencil and fill in the bridges freehand with an artist's brush, or tape off the area and fill in with paints.

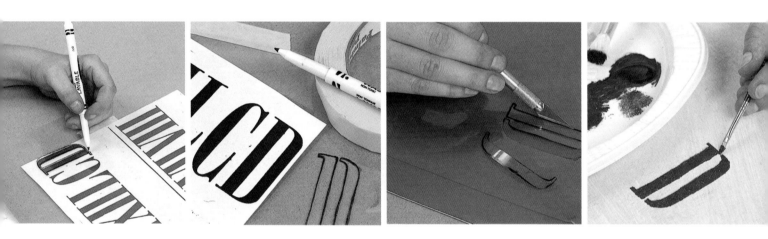

REPEATING A STENCIL PATTERN

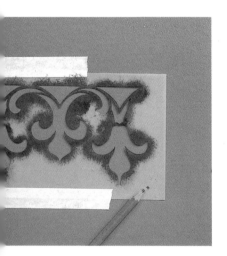

When working on a stenciled border with a repeat, such as trailing ivy or an architectural design, the length of the stencil should be one repeat, and the end of the stencil should be the same as the beginning. Small holes are cut as registration marks on either side of the stencil. When you are filling in the stencil border, add a little paint to the registration marks. When the stencil is moved to the left or right, realign the stencil over the holes.

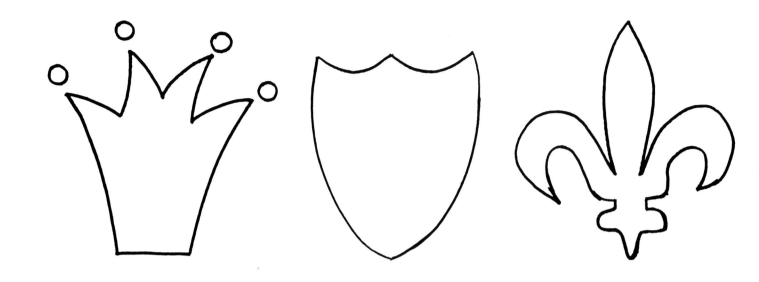

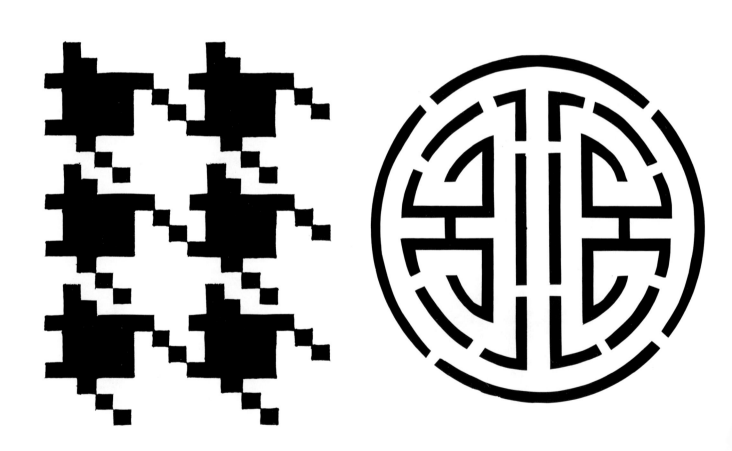

The outline for this shade is the template for the Spanish shade. To make that shade, enlarge this image on a photocopier to 125%.

Actual Size

resources

1. Design-A-Wall USA
199 Clifton Boulevard
P.O. Box 1988
Clifton, NJ 07015-1988
Tel: (973) 777-8305, (973) 777-1969
www.eastcoastweb.net/designawall
*Rubber rollers with stamped designs used
on the Damask Curtains.*

2. Graftek
P.O. Box 23260
Knoxville, TN 37933-1260
Tel: (423) 777-9480
Fax: (423) 777-9482
*Coloured Japan leaf and dry adhesive for
the Leafed Canvas Floorcloth.*

3. Hancock Shaker Village
P.O. Box 927
Pittsfield, MA 01202
Tel: (413) 443-0188
Fax: (413) 447-9357
www.hancockshakervillage.org
*Webbed seating for the Shaker Webbed
Seating.*

4. Hot Potatoes
2805 Columbine Place
Nashville, TN 37204
Tel: (615) 269-8002
Fax: (615) 269-8004
www.hotpotatoes.com
Feather stamp for Pressed Velvet Cushions.

5. Martin & Associates
139 Labrosse
Pointe Claire, Quebec
H9R 1A3 Canada
Tel: (514) 697-3000
Fax: (514) 697-4116
Stencils, specialty products.

6. Modern Options
2325 Third Street #339
San Francisco, CA 94107
Tel: (415) 252-5580
Fax: (415) 252-5599
www.modernoptions.com
*Mosaic supplies for Mosaic Garden Table;
metallic patinas.*

7. Montreal Decorators
251 Ste. Catherine East
Montreal, Quebec
H2X 1L5 Canada
Tel: (800) 215-6910
Specialty art and paint supply.

8. Ritins Studio Inc.
170 Wicksteed Avenue
Toronto, Ontario
M4G 2B6 Canada
Tel: (416) 467-8920
Fax: (416) 467-8963
www.ritins.com
*Venetian plaster for Plaster Barnwood
Shelves, ornamental gesso for the Bathroom
Cabinet Frame.*

Ritins Studio Inc. USA
C/o Modern Masters Inc.
7340 Greenbush Avenue
North Hollywood, CA 91605
Tel: (800) 942-3166, (818) 765-2915
Fax: (818) 765-0013
*Venetian plaster for Plaster Barnwood
Shelves, ornamental gesso for the Bathroom
Cabinet Frame.*

9. Steptoe & Wife Antiques
90 Tycos Drive
Toronto, Ontario
M6B 1V9 Canada
Tel: (800) 461-0060
www.steptoewife.com
Anaglypta for the Faux Leather Frame.

For more information and
help for any of your weekend
projects, visit our Web site at
www.painted-house.com.
And for more inspiration for
decorating your home, watch
Debbie Travis' Painted House.

index

DATE			